W9-AFC-048

ALMOST INNOCENT

ALMOST INNOCENT

From searching to saved
in America's criminal justice system

SHANTI BRIEN

"You never really understand a person until you consider things from his point of view . . . Until you climb inside of his skin and walk around in it."

-Harper Lee, *To Kill a Mockingbird*

www.amplifypublishing.com

Almost Innocent: From searching to saved in America's criminal justice system

For more information, please contact:
Amplify Publishing
620 Herndon Parkway, Suite 320
Herndon, VA 20170
info@amplifypublishing.com

Library of Congress Control Number: 2020900856

CPSIA Code: PRFRE2010A
ISBN-13: 978-1-64543-203-6

Printed in Canada

For Doug, my lifelong challenge and the love-of-my-life.

AUTHOR'S NOTE

These events actually happened. But, I have relied on my memory for many events, and as any good criminal defense lawyer will point out, memories are fallible. Most but not all names and identifying characteristics have been changed to disguise identities and protect families. The courtroom dialogue is from transcripts with only occasional minor changes for clarity. Some dialogue and events were recreated from trial transcripts because, of course, I couldn't attend all of my clients' crimes. Some conversations with clients were compressed from letters, meetings, and phone calls.

PROLOGUE

"**I** need a lawyer," my husband said.

I stopped walking. I stood still in the rush of mothers hurrying up the shady hill from our kids' school.

"Are you there?" he said. "I need an attorney."

I pressed the phone a little harder to my ear. It was confusing. Because I *am* an attorney.

I'm a criminal defense lawyer. I do appeals. When you've lost at trial, when you're facing eighty-seven-years-to-life in a cement cage with a metal toilet, that's when you need me. When Doug needs me, it's to decide what to put into the planter bed in front; it's to pick out some new cool jeans; it's to remind him to slow down and come home, the kids will be gone soon.

Doug and I have been married for seventeen years. For ten of those, he was a placekicker in the NFL. In our football days, Doug needed me to cheer at all of the games and to spend lazy Tuesday mornings cozied up in bed with him. Later, he would need me to get up with the babies so he could rest for the next game. Now that he runs a real estate company and our three kids are a little older, he calls to ask if I can meet him for dinner with a big client or if I can bring the bag of balls to the soccer field for Zach's practice. He doesn't need legal advice. He has an army of corporate lawyers, available at any time for $800 an hour.

"You need an attorney?" I asked, the words sounding strange.

He was quiet. I imagined him standing at his office window, looking down onto Lake Merritt; how clean and blue it looked from twenty-four stories above. I imagined him nodding, not quite able to speak, and—because he said nothing—I knew we were in trouble.

Some of my clients are innocent. Some claim innocence. Many enter into years of deliberation over a minute legal error, the mistake that will set them free or cost them their lives. The overwhelming truth is the same for every person involved in criminal proceedings: the system is messy, confusing, costly, and often, in the end, disastrous. Even for the innocent. Especially for the innocent.

My husband had to be innocent.

"Do you remember Lance, that guy that worked on the courthouse steps?"

I flashed back to a barbeque in our backyard. The whole company had been there—all twelve or so employees, their spouses, and kids. Lance slid in late. He'd worn long surfer shorts, hair slicked back, and he'd brought his young kids, his mother-in-law, and his wife. She stood several inches taller than him in tight white jeans, platform shoes, platinum blonde hair, and a fairly good-sized boob job.

"The feds are looking at him for collusion. For taking money to not bid on houses," Doug said.

"He did a lot of work for you."

Lance had been the go-to guy for buying houses at auctions for Doug's company. Every week, Lance touched down at "courthouse steps" all across the Bay Area counties, hundreds of thousands of dollars in cashier's checks flying from his pockets, to scoop up the foreclosed houses being auctioned off to the highest bidder. The feds thought that Lance and the other guys on the steps were paying each other to *stop* bidding on the houses their funders wanted. Funders like Doug and Doug's friend, Steve.

SHANTI BRIEN

"Steve just called me. He was in his office and got served. There were a bunch of companies listed, and ours is one of them. I guess they subpoenaed every company that bought properties in the last couple of years. He told me to lawyer up."

"He worked with Lance, too?"

"Some other guy. But all of them were kind of shady."

"This is . . . serious."

I knew the feds were cracking down hard on all types of mortgage fraud. This subpoena was one little piece of a huge national investigation. Like the stock back-dating scandal a few years prior, I knew that for some people, a subpoena could become criminal charges. Even if Doug hadn't planned the scheme, if he'd given Lance the money knowing where it was actually going, that could be a crime. My husband could face criminal charges: mail fraud, wire fraud, bank fraud, I didn't know exactly which, but each violation would be ten years in prison and a million-dollar fine. *Each violation.* Lance had bought over 100 houses for Doug's company.

"I need you," Doug said, "to help me find an attorney."

In a way (though prospective criminal charges brought us to a new level), this phone call fit our normal course of business. Doug forged ahead with superhuman determination, relentless perseverance, and a fairy tale "I can do anything" attitude. There was no thought of consequences or collateral damage. I put on the brakes, I pulled the reins, I served up the prescription-strength dose of realism, and I cleaned up the mess. It had been this way since day five of our marriage.

| | | | |

I was sweating like I was in a spin class in a heat wave in Death Valley. Rivers of perspiration formed below me on the dirt path. Sweat stung my eyes and blurred my vision. I blindly swerved my bike over the rocks and scrubby plants along the path. This was my honeymoon.

Doug had painstakingly planned this trip. He had also tested every morsel of the organic meals prepared by the wedding caterers and sampled the wines to create the best "pairings." I'd done the rest. We'd arrived in Belize predictably exhausted. Doug, though, could not wait to show me La Placencia Peninsula. The scant information provided by the new World Wide Web promised "unspoiled" natural beauty and "undeveloped" relaxation. I learned this was tourism-code for no restaurants, pools, or basic first-world infrastructure.

Whenever I forced myself to look up from the bike's gears, I could make out the vague outline of Doug (mostly his cute butt and his strong back) riding ahead. He was fit, of course; his athletic legs casually worked the pedals. First, he was 50 yards ahead, then 100. He finally looked over his shoulder, his black hair messy and his smile wide and white. He made a quick U-turn and pedaled back.

"How are things going back here?"

I stopped my bike. "When I thought of my honeymoon . . ."

The heat settled around me, and my brain couldn't form the words.

"I didn't think I'd want to puke," I finally spat.

What I didn't tell him was that I really wanted to kick his ass. And then sleep. And then lounge by a clean pool with cute waiters who would bring me piña coladas and spritz me with restorative mineral water.

We had been hitting the adventure hard. We'd kayaked a couple miles in the morning and hiked to the Mayan ruins in the afternoon sun. We'd jogged on the beach in the morning, canoed through the mangroves in the afternoon. Snorkeled in the morning, biked up a mountain in the afternoon. On this fifth day, I wanted to collapse.

"Oh, baby." Doug handed me a warm bottle of water and wiped my face with his shirt. "You didn't tell me!"

"Of course I didn't."

I wanted to be a cool, fun wife. I wanted us to have a unique, exciting honeymoon. I wanted Doug to feel proud of his plans and love me for loving it all.

"What do you want to do? Just tell me."

"I want to sit on a lounge chair in the shade with an orange Fanta. I want to relax and listen to the jungle."

"Then we'll do that."

And we did. He found a pair of beautiful wooden lounge chairs and pulled them into the shade of the thatched bungalow. From the veranda, I could see glimpses of the river through the dense green jungle. Doug delivered an icy Fanta in the quintessential Central American recycled glass bottle. As much as he loved those reach-the-peak adventures, gritty workouts, and thigh-burning rides, he loved me more.

For the rest of our marriage, Doug has displayed the perseverance of an ultra-marathoner and the energy of a quadruple espresso; I stumble behind, sometimes pissed but always exhausted. Often, I let him think I'm loving the ride. It was this way with the NFL, as he extended his kicking career through extra workouts and extraordinary mental training, through twelve years of moving around the country, switching teams and homes and friends with every move. It was this way with our three kids. He could be up with the crying toddler half the night, make peanut butter omelets in the morning for hungry girls, have four networking meetings for his new business, and still lead the under-six neighborhood kids in the Paramount Road Soccer Club in the afternoon.

I am the parent who opens a bottle of wine, slumps onto the sofa, and says, "Sure, let's turn on another episode of *Modern Family*." My role is to slow things down, to want less, to follow the rules, and to enjoy today without always working so hard to get to the next accomplishment.

But now, the gritty residue of Doug's high-performance life had invaded his business. He had forged ahead on this new company with such speed and determination that he had left a trail behind him of sweaty mishaps, exhausted employees, and a tired wife.

At the very beginning of the mortgage crisis, Doug had bought a small bungalow near our home in Northern California; a few months later, a townhouse and a couple of ranch-style homes. He remodeled, then rented them. In the first year, he had bought 130 homes and raised enough private investments to buy about 200 more. In some areas of Northern California, his company turned whole neighborhoods around. Run-down foreclosed homes with weeds three-feet high and broken windows became beautiful homes for working families. He drove this business at 200 miles an hour. And three years later, it crashed into the United States Justice Department.

There was no jungle shade and no drink—no matter how strong—to fix this.

I knew the bleak path through the criminal justice system. In my work, I witness hope and resilience; I see gratitude and self-awareness. But mostly, I lose, and my clients lose. When people hire me, they have lost at trial; they have been sentenced to prison or are already incarcerated. They write to me on scraps of paper with nubs of pencils, hoping I can create an argument strong enough to succeed where another attorney failed. The system is set up so that their convictions are upheld, and we lose. Convictions should be upheld, or else the justice system would explode with re-trials. So, I defend a young kid who's been put away for life for being the passenger in the wrong car at the wrong time. I work really hard, and then, almost always, we lose.

With this mindset, I found my family faced with a subpoena from United States Justice Department that could lead to years of investigation. I saw criminal history points—three for no "acceptance of responsibility" by fighting the charges at a trial, two for using "sophisticated means," four for being a "leader"—which added up to more than ten years in prison. After ten years, our girls would be nearly out of college; Zach would be a teenager. Doug would miss high school proms and game-winning soccer goals, every holiday, every birthday party, every family dinner around our worn-in, banged-up, beautiful farm table. I had visions of degrading headlines in the papers focused on Doug's missed kicks years ago and his missing morals today. I could picture the woman who lived down the street looking at me with disgust and pity, wondering if it was appropriate to bring a lasagna to a woman whose husband is in prison. My hardworking, justice-upholding attorney-self and my dutiful-wife-and-mother-self were crashing together into a giant heap of crazy.

This was, most fundamentally and in a way that felt so humbling, supposed to happen to other people. Like my clients. I had already given up so much for Doug's success, and I was about to be buried in his wake again. I had survived a mentally ill, absent father, the roller coaster of the NFL, and 1,000 visits to Gymboree. But what were our chances in this grinding system of injustice that had defeated so many? This memoir is the story of my search for answers—answers for my family, but also the answers that undergird our legal system. It is the story of my clients: men and women, sons and daughters, guilty and innocent, old and young, white and brown and black. This is the story of their attorney: part brown and part white, young but growing up, daughter of an unstable father and a single mother, wife of an NFL player, mother of three, and fighter for justice. This is the story of my journey through the criminal justice system: colossal mistakes, a few appellate victories, and the dead body of a middle-aged father in Santa Rita County Jail.

CHAPTER 1

FATHERS-AND-LAW

I stood next to the mother of young Nick Yang and her two companions in the long hallway of the Ninth Circuit Court of Appeals—the last stop in the federal court system before the United States Supreme Court. We were practically entombed in marble: floors, walls, ceiling. A chill moved through me from the gleaming rock and from nervousness. Even after almost ten years of representing people in their appeals, the magnitude of the predicament, the knowledge that I was my client's last chance, and the sheer, echoey weight of the courtrooms made the Ninth Circuit just plain scary.

If standing, Nick's mother would have barely reached my shoulder. But she sat on a bench, hunched. Her companions were strikingly beautiful Hmong women in their early twenties; both had perfectly-straightened, long, black hair and short, black skirts. One was my client's sister, one his "friend." (Friends don't wait out a sentence of seventy-two-years-to-life.) Nick's dad had died a few years before; his mother was alone and scared. The weight of the day and the fate of her eldest child weighed heavy on her shoulders.

For all the important cases that moved through that court, for all the lives on the line, it was strangely quiet. Down the hall, a gray security guard in a blue jacket whispered people through the door and the metal detector, but we could hardly hear him.

I spoke softly, telling the women what to expect in court. It was my standard opening. Nick's sister translated for their mom.

"I will get ten minutes to discuss the case with the panel of judges. Three judges will sit on the bench. They will ask questions. I will address the questions, and then the Attorney General will have ten minutes. You will not get a chance to talk."

The mother looked bewildered and sad.

"What are our chances?" she asked, through her daughter.

I had been asked this so many times, by so many desperate people, and yet I could not be totally honest.

"This is an uphill battle. It's how the system is set up." Nick's chances were near zero, but I could not help myself: "I'm still hopeful."

The mother began to cry. "My baby," she whimpered.

| | | | |

I remember watching my mom cry as she read the letter from my father. I couldn't have been more than five. We sat in the Raley's parking lot, in the height of the Central Valley summer heat, bare thighs sticking to the car's seats. We cranked the windows down, but not even a hint of a breeze accepted the invitation.

We hadn't seen my father in a few years. He had finally written to us, to say that he was living in Southern California, interested in artificial intelligence, and working with dolphins. I imagined the cool water of the dolphin pool; it sounded so nice. My father seemed smart and important, like a trainer at Marine World. I fantasized that he performed groundbreaking work in a faraway place; that's why he couldn't come see me.

My mom couldn't be bothered with dolphins. She must have been worried about paying for the groceries or finding our next rental. She lived in a daze of exhaustion from working two or three part-time jobs and heartbreak from my dad leaving her.

For my birthday that year, he came back.

I skipped up to Maw-maw and Paw-paw's door. Maw-maw and Paw-paw were my father's parents; even though my father had left my mom when I was still a baby, Maw-maw and Paw-paw took care of me and treated my mom like part of the family.

I used the same names for them that my father had used for his grandparents back in Oklahoma. That was the Okie way. My grandmother was Muscogee; she'd grown up in a tiny town in Indian Country, on the allotment given to her family when the government tried to "civilize" the Muscogee/Creek tribe by forcing them onto private farms from their communal lands. Paw-paw grew up in the same town, on a ranch with a big white house, a barn, and tractors. My grandparents lived out a cowboy-Indian romance, and the young couple rode off into the West. They came to the fertile Central Valley of California to seek a new life for themselves and their first baby—my father, Hal.

My mom had grown up in Hawaii to extraordinary but Haole parents. Her dad was the first pathologist on the islands, and her mother was a paraplegic who, at the age of thirty-five, began having a family. My mother was the first child. When the fifth arrived with Down syndrome, the whole family moved to the Central Valley so he could get the services he needed.

My grandfather hadn't liked anything about my mom's decision to marry a hippie Indian when she was only twenty, so he'd disowned her. She went to Modesto Junior College and baked pies for a little cash. Her mother helped, but Maw-maw and Paw-paw were like my parents. He taught me to read and play checkers; she took me to dentist appointments and sewed my clothes.

The day of my fifth birthday, I wore my short shorts and a little floral halter top Maw-maw had sewn for me. I couldn't wait to see what I'd get for my birthday. Maw-maw always got me the best clothes—special, because they were store-bought or she had embroidered my name on the front—but what I really wanted was that Barbie DreamHouse.

I pushed through the front door. It seemed strange and kind of dark. The cool of the air conditioner felt like a slap on my warm, bare shoulders. Everyone turned to me, smiling. Aunt Dana, Uncle Jesse—even Maw-maw's little dog Tammy yipped and jumped up, her paws leaving red marks on my bare legs. Maw-maw shushed Tammy out the sliding glass doors, as if her yipping were the problem. The dog wasn't the problem.

The problem was the man sitting in the recliner by the door. He was dressed up like a clown, in a wig with bright orange-red braids, a polka dot tie, and white face makeup with a large, red, painted-on smile. The white, though, had smudged, and his dark skin showed through. The braids kept falling in his eyes, and he slowly pushed them aside. He just sat there with his painted smile.

"Surprise!" they shouted.

They laughed. They smiled at each other with looks that said, "Isn't this great?" and "She's so surprised!" Maw-maw expected me to do something or say something, but I didn't know what she wanted.

I turned to my mom. She stood back by the door. I walked to her and grabbed her leg. She didn't know what to do any more than I did. She was twenty-six years old, a single mom on food stamps, and here was Hal, the love of her life. She hadn't seen him in years; she definitely hadn't received any child support. My grown-up mother would probably call him an "asshole" and walk out, but that afternoon, the pain was too fresh.

"Don't be shy, Shanti," someone said to me. "This special clown is here to celebrate your birthday."

I knew he was my father. I don't know how I knew, but I did.

"Go ahead and sit on his lap, Shanti. He is so nice."

I worried that Maw-maw would be disappointed, that my Aunt Dana would be angry, though I wasn't sure why. All I knew was that I did not want to sit on that man's lap. I wanted my mom to pick me up and carry me back out into the light and heat of the Modesto summer, where Tammy was barking to be let back in.

My mom reached her hand down to my bare shoulder. Just the slightest hint of a nudge. I inched toward the strange man. I stood by him.

Quietly, I said, "Hello."

"Today's your birthday!" His voice was soft but forced.

I didn't want to, but I let him pick me up and set me on his lap.

"You are such a beautiful young lady. Isn't this the happiest of days?"

But I could hear it in his voice, and I could see it in his eyes: he wasn't happy at all.

| | | | |

About a year before I met Nick's mom in the marble hallway of the Ninth Circuit, I'd sat with Nick himself at a linoleum table in the visiting room of Folsom State Prison. He was twenty-three, short, skinny, and swimming in baggy jeans and the chambray shirt that every prisoner wore buttoned all the way up. With his black hair cropped short and dark, wide-set eyes, he could have passed for a teenager.

When I'd extended my hand in greeting and he'd lifted his, we'd both heard the snap of the heavy steel chain connecting his hands to his waist.

On the cold benches, we talked quietly to avoid the guards. I told Nick about myself, mixed bits about Stanford and Berkeley, growing up in the Central Valley. I'd lived most of my life right down Highway 99 from where we sat talking. Then, I asked him to tell me about himself.

"My family is Hmong, from the mountains of Laos. My father came to Dallas after fighting alongside the US in the Vietnam War. I was the first of ten kids. When I was around four, my parents followed our relatives to the Central Valley. My parents didn't speak much English. We were poor. In a bad neighborhood."

I told him that my mother still lived in Merced, not far from where she'd raised me. A good number of her students at the junior college where she taught child development were Hmong.

"We lived in a pretty big apartment complex with a lot of Hmong people, sixty or seventy families, maybe more. It was like a little Hmongtown; everyone looked out for each other. People just had their doors wide open all day, even after dark. Always music playing. Kids got to run around all over the place. People gardened in the big, empty field. It was huge, the garden. Like the ones I heard about in Asia. It was like a jungle maze. We loved running around in there."

I imagined a skinny kid racing through lush gardens with his friends, pretending they were in the mountains of Laos rather than the deadening summer heat of the Valley.

"But in the streets . . ." Something shifted, and Nick got serious. "There were always gangsters. All day, all night, in and out."

"You got involved with them?"

"My grades were good. I liked school. A lot. I was really good at math. Easily my favorite subject. Teacher had to give me math books that were two to three levels higher. But junior high wasn't so good. All the different crowds made it seem like I had to belong to one. My friends were either hanging around gangs or straight-up gang members. I got a lot of attention from girls."

For a moment, he looked very far away, like he was remembering something even more clearly. "I saw a lot of fights. People stabbed, shot, and killed."

"You felt you had no choice, that you had to get involved?"

"My gang was KONG, and it was about power. With power comes fame, money, and girls."

This was honesty. I was impressed. Really, a lot of us are concerned about accomplishment and recognition, money, and sex—we just don't admit it so openly. But a life-sentence has that effect on people; they have nothing to lose by being honest.

"When I got in, around 1994, KONG was already the biggest, strongest gang. Not just in the Valley. In other cities around the US." He flashed with something like pride. "But things got bad."

Nick looked down at the linoleum, a scratch of graffiti.

He was quiet for so long that I shifted in my seat. I wasn't afraid of him. Not exactly. He seemed harmless and was probably in prison for at least my lifetime. But gangs scared me. Asian gangs in the Central Valley have terrorized so many people. I try to be careful about my privacy: I have mail sent to a post office box, I don't advertise my physical address or post pictures of my kids on social media. Still, gangs had their ways. I imagined Nick's rival members finding me days after he was set free, a carload of them driving slowly down the leafy street in front of my Oakland home.

Nick told me he got shot once in the hip; he felt lucky to be alive.

"I knew they would hurt my family one day. I was trying to get out when everything went down."

| | | | |

"Head to Steinway?" Pao paged Nick.

Nick loved playing basketball at Steinway Park. He and his friends played there almost every day. He drove to pick up Pao.

As Pao got into the car, he threw a black gun on Nick's lap. He kept a silver one for himself. "For safety."

"I don't need this."

But Nick left it in his lap. He wouldn't mess around with Pao. Pao belonged to KONG down south, and had been locked up in the California Youth Authority for shootings there. They drove around, picking up their friends Cha and Tou.

"We're in, but one sec," Cha said through the open window of the car. "Money just rolled in. He gotta drop some weed before he goes back."

"We'll follow you. Then Steinway," said Nick.

On the way to the park, Nick got a page from his friend Kelly. He thought he saw her in a car going the other way, just after a blue Honda Prelude. Nick made a U-turn, but she was gone.

"I'm gonna see if her friends know where she's going."

Nick pulled up across from the park, driving slowly.

"Pull over there," someone in the car said. "By that blue Honda."

"This is KONG!" Pao yelled out the open window. "I said, this is KONG."

The kids in the blue Prelude didn't say anything. Nick didn't recognize them as rivals. He wasn't sure why Pao was yelling.

"They might have guns," Tou said.

Then, fireworks. Blasts of heat and smoke. Car doors blurred open, people ran and screamed. Something was burning.

In slow motion, Nick inched out of the car, black gun in hand. Pao fired the silver gun four times into the Honda's windshield and driver's door. In the back seat, a teenage girl hunched over and screamed and screamed and screamed. The driver fell on the steering wheel, his head slick and black with blood. Another kid, in basketball shorts and a T-shirt, lay on the sidewalk behind the car; his basketball rolled into the grass.

Nick jumped back into the car and threw the black gun at Pao.

"Why the fuck are there still bullets in this gun, man? Why you run out the car for, if you didn't step out to shoot?"

"The gun," Nick said. "It—it jammed."

Later that day, at just eighteen years old, Nick Yang was arrested for a shooting he didn't commit.

| | | | |

"Did the gun jam?" I asked him in the faded visitor room.

"You know? No."

He looked over to the guard sitting in the cubicle, then back to the table. He lifted his dark eyes.

"I ran because I didn't want to get shot again. I didn't want to get shot, and I didn't want to shoot anybody, neither."

The prosecutor had charged Nick with a slew of crimes and sentencing enhancements (extra time for particularly bad offenses, like using a gun and being in a gang). Conviction on all the charges totaled up to about 100 years in prison.

The prosecutor had pressed everyone to admit their involvement and identify the shooter. Tou pled guilty. He'd told police at the scene that Pao was the shooter. But because he was so scared of Pao, Tou refused to testify under oath at Nick's trial.

Pao also agreed to a deal—a great deal. But it wouldn't be complete until after Nick's trial.

The prosecutor was putting forth the theory that Nick was the shooter; he didn't want that messed up. He wanted to be able to revoke any of the plea deals if someone decided to testify on Nick's behalf and say that Pao Ma was the shooter. The prosecutor admitted that he made the same arrangement in all of the plea bargains in the case.

He was bold enough to tell the judge, "I did not want anybody to come into court and testify without having any repercussions. If Pao Ma got on the stand and testified that he was the shooter, then fine. Let's do that. But Pao wasn't getting immunity. Later, when his [judgment and sentencing] came along, he'd have to suffer the consequences . . . possibly have his plea withdrawn."

The judge, who'd seen hundreds of cases in almost fifty years on the bench, asked the prosecutor, "Are you concerned that the appellate court would frown upon plea agreements that had the effect of preventing witnesses from testifying?"

"No," the prosecutor said simply. "If they wanted to get up there and testify, they could. They'd deal with the consequences."

The consequences for Pao were that the fourteen years he'd won in his plea bargain would suddenly be at least fifty. No one was willing to have their deal revoked.

At Nick's trial, the prosecutor presented several contradictory stories from witnesses (including Nick's friends in the car behind him). Although some witnesses testified that they thought the driver fired the shots, others said that the passenger, Pao Ma, had. Nick took the stand and told the jury exactly what had happened. He jumped out of the car and he had a gun, but he didn't shoot anyone. He never intended to.

In closing arguments, the prosecutor, knowing that he had made deals to prevent Pao and Tou from testifying that Pao was the real shooter, said:

So, what do we have? We got witnesses that say the defendant, the driver of that vehicle, either shot at the blue car or shot at [one victim]. Why? Because this man was the shooter. It was [Nick's] show. This person was the executioner. It's a simple case. That's why I'm not going to talk very long. It's a simple case. These are simple facts. It's all about [Nick].

The jury deliberated for five long days. (Some juries in murder cases consider the evidence for an hour or two before returning a guilty verdict.) This jury asked the court to replay testimony several times from the witnesses who said the driver was the shooter. But ultimately, the jury found Nick guilty. They decided he was the shooter and should be punished as such.

A few months later, Pao Ma pled guilty and was sentenced. At that point, Pao and Tou agreed to tell their stories. Their plea deals had already won them favorable sentences, and the prosecutor could not take that away. Nick's attorney asked for a new trial to present Pao's and Tou's testimony. In the hearing on whether there should be a new trial, the judge listened to Pao and Tou testify under oath.

Pao Ma's story corroborated Nick's. He said they originally followed the Prelude to the park because Nick thought he knew a girl in the car ahead of the Prelude. Pao claimed that when they arrived, he and Tou got out of the car to ask the passengers in the Prelude what gang they belonged to.

"I got out with the gun, went out there, asked the one guy— there was a guy that came out of the car. I asked him where you from, what gang you claim, and he ran to the back of the—his car. I seen the driver of his car, of the other Prelude car, and I shot him," Pao testified.

I imagine silence settled over the courtroom, that even the court reporter paused her typing for a second.

"Did you shoot at the guy who was out of the car, too?" the prosecutor asked.

"Yes," Pao said.

"Did you hit him?"

"Yes."

"Did you see him go down?"

"Yes."

"Total number of shots, how many were fired?"

"Seven."

"Okay. Did you fire all seven shots?"

"Yes."

"Did the people in the Prelude do anything to attract your attention? Flash gang signs? Anything like that?"

"No. Just the car. For me, personally, it was the car, the way the car was. It was a low rider, stuff like that. They was Asian."

Tou told the same story. He added that when Nick returned to the car, he said his gun had jammed. Nick hadn't mentioned this in his testimony. It would become a crucial fact.

Considering this new testimony, the judge found that there was "a reasonable probability of a different result on the issue of who fired the gun." The judge thought that Pao fired the shots, not Nick. But this was not enough for a new trial. The judge found that the verdicts would probably have been the same, even with the new testimony. Some evidence showed that Nick at least aided Pao. He drove the car. He slowed the car next to the Prelude. The judge reasoned that if Nick said his gun had jammed, that meant he had tried to shoot someone. Without a new trial, there was no way Nick could explain that he only had said the gun jammed because Pao was angry that he hadn't fired.

Even though he denied Nick's motion for a new trial, the judge made it very clear on the record, for the prosecutor and for the Court of Appeal who would eventually read every word of the proceedings, that he did not approve of the prosecutor's methods, the way he'd made plea bargains contingent on *not* testifying. Pao had no real choice whether to testify at Nick's trial. He was willing to tell the truth, but he wasn't crazy. Not even an honest and regretful gang member (and no one thought Pao was that) would have given away fourteen years to get fifty-to-life.

The judge let the prosecutor choose between a new trial or a reduced sentence for Nick. The prosecutor took the sentencing reduction, which was much more secure than a new trial with all that new evidence. The judge removed some sentencing enhancements and kept the remaining verdicts in place, sentencing Nick to sixty-five-years-to-life plus seven years.

Nick will first be eligible for parole after serving seventy-two years.

Pao Ma received a sentence of fourteen years and was released after ten.

I had come into Nick's life—appointed by the court—when his case finally reached the Ninth Circuit. He'd already directly appealed in the California Court of Appeal and petitioned the California Supreme Court to review the case. He was denied.

Then, he moved on to the "Great Writ," the writ of habeas corpus. In Latin, habeas corpus means "you have a body." A writ of habeas corpus is used to bring a prisoner before the court to challenge the legal basis for restraining a prisoner's body against his will. A habeas petition is technically a civil action, like a lawsuit against your old landlord for not returning your security deposit. It's not officially an extension of the criminal case, like an appeal. Like suing the landlord, the prisoner brings the lawsuit against the state agent who holds him—the warden of the prison—claiming that the warden is imprisoning him illegally.

In California, attorneys generally use habeas petitions to bring the court's attention to evidence that was not presented at trial. An appeal is limited to events that happened at the trial, the papers that the attorneys filed, and the transcript of what was said in court. Collectively, everything that happened at the trial is contained in "the record," those written and bound documents. Sometimes, however, your "corpus" is thrown in a dirty prison because of something that happened outside of the record: a witness lied but now wants to recant, your attorney made a horrible mistake, the prosecutor never revealed evidence in your favor.

For instance, in an appeal, I might challenge a judge's instruction to the jury about vandalism:

To prove that the defendant is guilty of felony vandalism, the People must prove that: The defendant maliciously defaced with *graffiti, damaged or destroyed property and the amount of damage was $400 or more.*

The judge forgot the part about the defendant not owning the property, alone or with others. This is important; it prevents vandalism convictions when your five-year-old child inscribes her name in your antique dining room table with the broken end of a ballpoint pen, or your husband paints an "accent" wall in the living room a ridiculous shade of burgundy. Both violations could cause damage over $400 (the threshold for a felony). But since the offenders basically own the property, they are not guilty of a crime, despite the felony-level upset.

On the other hand, in a habeas petition challenging my conviction for child neglect (I have not been convicted of child neglect, but just for the sake of illustration, if I *were*), I could present evidence, in the form of a signed declaration from my friend Erin—one that had not been submitted during the trial—that even though I was technically not at home with the kids and technically I was drinking vodka, cranberry, and Fresca cocktails at her house across the street, I had the monitor on and was listening intently for any sign of immediate distress. I would also submit a declaration from my attorney admitting that he had no strategic reason for failing to call Erin to testify in my defense at my trial.

In federal court, the habeas petition must address constitutional violations. Nick's case was flush with constitutional violations. The deprivation of his right to present witnesses in his defense violated Nick's fundamental due process and compulsory process rights under the Fifth and Sixth Amendments. The ineffective assistance of counsel in addressing the plea-bargaining scheme created by the prosecutor also violated Nick's Sixth Amendment right to counsel.

Nick made these arguments in three petitions for writ of habeas corpus in the California Superior Court, the Court of Appeal, and the California Supreme Court. They were denied.

After a habeas petition to the federal district court was also denied, the Ninth Circuit decided there *was* something to consider. They asked me to handle it.

When I met Nick, he had been behind bars for thirteen years. He told me in a letter:

I remember a time I thought my dad was proud of me when I was in the ninth grade. The high school enrolled me in the Navy's R.O.T.C. program. They issued us real Navy uniforms to wear for certain days on campus. My dad was so proud when he saw me in uniform; he took pictures to send back to his brothers in Laos. It must've been disappointing to him when I later got expelled from school after a gang fight.

Two years ago, he passed away of diabetes. Some said that my incarceration helped kill him and I believe it. He used to be so full and healthy but when I got locked up, time just ate away at him.

Time and depression ate away at my father too.

I was twelve-and-a-half and hadn't seen him since he dressed up as a clown for my fifth birthday. That spring afternoon, Maw-maw picked me up from school to tell me he had moved back. She and Paw-paw wanted me to see him. We drove out a long country road, the back way to Turlock. We passed small family farms and almond orchards, endless rows of trees flashing by the backseat window. The apartment complex was a collection of gray, one-story buildings surrounded by carports full of old cars and pick-ups. A beat-up ten-speed bike hunched in the corner by his front door.

When my father opened the gray door, he didn't have the painted-on smile; his black hair was tied in a ponytail. The dark apartment behind him reminded me of my birthday. A futon lay folded in the corner of the room, blankets and pillows stacked neatly on top. Pencil drawings and small paintings lined the base-boards, a few even thumbtacked to the walls. On a small table sat piles of papers and math books.

He gave us a tour of the art. His intricate pencil drawings looked like photographs. He showed us one of Martha, a thin bal-lerina, looking to the left so that the tendons in her neck seemed to come off of the paper; another of a sailboat catching the wind, moving quickly across rough seas. These were his life without me, his life in sunny Southern California. I didn't understand why, but I knew that his life there had turned bad. Somehow, I had always known that Hal had once been a promising student at Cal Tech; before that, his high school's handsome student body president.

Years later, I found out that Martha, the side-glancing ballerina, had called Maw-maw and Paw-paw in the middle of the night to tell them that Hal had run off to Mexico. Could they come down and find him, try to help him?

They could. They did. They found him and brought him back to Modesto, but they could never save him from his own sadness. Neither could I. It always felt too precarious. From the time I was twelve—from even before then, when I was five, sitting on his clown lap—I understood that he was a man who could disappear at any moment, disintegrate. He would leave me. Soon after I saw him in his dark apartment, he was diagnosed with depression. This would become entirely consuming, the story of the rest of his life.

| | | | |

In the marble hallway of the Ninth Circuit, waiting with Nick's family before the oral argument, I imagined Nick locked in a small cage for the rest of his life, the real shooter having walked free a few years ago. Beside me, Nick's mother was bent over cry-ing. I knew the best way to help Nick and his mother.

I buttoned my black jacket and told her with certainty and firmness, "I promise I am doing my absolute best for your son. We need to go into court now."

CHAPTER 2

THE PRESUMPTION OF INNOCENCE

O n the drive to meet David Tuggle—my new client, a convicted rapist serving a three-strikes sentence for drug possession—I noticed the rolling golden hills, the sweep of highway-side electrical lines, and the old oaks creating patches of black shade on the hillsides.

Nice place for a picnic or some icy lemonade, I thought.

But I couldn't stop. I needed to make it to Folsom State Prison before officials began the prisoner count at 11:00 am.

Four times every day, Folsom, just like every prison, counts the inmates to make sure they have everyone. I've never found it reassuring that institutions feel the need to engage in a simple headcount several times each day, but that's the way prisons are—paranoid. There can be no movement during that time, no visitors, and spending those forty-five minutes in the blazing parking lot wasn't part of my plan.

My conversation with David Tuggle wasn't going to be a brief one. His habeas petition and briefs had been denied by the federal district court. The petition was so bloated with legal arguments, fifty pages of handwritten legal jargon and case names, that I could hardly make out the points he was making. I knew the Ninth Circuit showed the most interest in his claim that his twenty-five-years-to-life sentence under the three-strikes law for possession of one dose of drugs was excessive. It seemed excessive to me, too, but I wanted to talk to Mr. Tuggle about the rapes that made up his first two strikes. The rapes that happened not far from where I grew up in the Central Valley. The rapes he swore he didn't do.

Pulling off the highway, dry heat shimmered up from the pavement. It didn't help that I was wearing long, dark pants (no chambray or blue like the inmates) and a cream-colored blouse (no khaki or dark green like the guards). I was bummed I'd forgotten my non-underwire bra. This would surely cause a delay at the visitor's check-in. The metal detector's alarm would sound, and if the security guard was a man, he would need to call for a female guard to pat me down. She would lecture me on the dangers that wire could cause if it got into the hands of an inmate. I would apologize, and she would say, "Just this one time."

I arrived at the visitor check-in station. The young guard was loaded down with his essentials: gun, baton, taser, tear gas, and a bulletproof vest. I whipped out my ID and Bar card.

"Legal visit," I told him.

I had sent the prison my entire numerical life in advance, short of my children's birth dates and heights and weights: my Social Security Number, driver's license number, Bar number, address, phone number, and case number. He checked the paperwork and called for my escort.

Another big, young guy entered. He walked slowly under the weight of the weapons, the heat, and the bulletproof vest. It was so hot, he couldn't bear to walk the hundred yards to the prison gate.

"Let's catch a ride," he said.

So, we climbed in a golf cart. Across a field of black pavement, I saw the main prison.

Folsom rises out of the golden hills like a decaying castle. Stone walls and iron gates give it the look of a fortress. This is an old-school prison, built when the state was interested in the look of "security." Modern prisons, hardly more than concrete boxes, focus on sensory deprivation. Although Old Folsom is run-down, the turrets nestled in the oaks carry a certain charm. It even has a museum for tourists, filled with the ingenious weapons made by inmates and confiscated over the years. I've never stopped in, but would love to find the shiv made of an underwire.

We entered a cramped, dark room in the turret of the building. I signed the visitors' log, a dingy piece of paper on a clipboard, and joined the other two lawyers and a psychologist ahead of me on the list. I showed my ID and visitor's badge to another guard in a cramped cage. Bulletproof glass surrounded her with a small opening for exchanging passes. She wore her hair in a tight bun, the fashion for most female guards. In the small, dark room, she sat before monitors, dials, speakers, and buttons—not unlike the cockpit of a plane. A wall of enormous skeleton keys lined the wall behind her, remnants of the 1880s when the prison first opened.

After a long quarter-hour, she called my name and pressed a button to release the heavy, metal door. My escort and I stepped into the blazing heat.

For a moment, I felt like an inmate. Fences twenty feet high and topped with barbed wire surrounded us on three sides. As soon as the door slammed shut behind us, the gate in the fence began opening slowly. My escort gave a nod to the armed guards in the towers above us, and we stepped through.

I entered the visiting room. My escort checked in with the guard perched above the visiting floor as I took in the cracked linoleum floor. The walls were several shades of dirty off-white. A large mural adorned one wall. Probably painted by inmates years ago, it depicted green rolling hills, a shimmering pond, and some cattle. A mishmash of handwritten and officially-printed signs read:

"A kiss may be exchanged at the beginning and end of the visit only."

"No embracing. Holding hands is permitted above the table only."

"Visitors only may use vending machines; no inmates allowed."

I waited in a tiny interview room, no bigger than a small bathroom. A metal door led to the general visiting room; it had a window with wire mesh.

I guess the officers need to see if he attacks me, I thought.

The officer instructed me to sit in the rear of the room, my back almost against the wall; my client would sit with his back to the window. Strange, because I could get trapped there in the corner by a hulking, lunging prisoner.

I had asked the correctional officer for privacy. Sex offenders are the dregs of the prison. Child molestation would be the worst offense imaginable, in terms of an inmate's safety, but a prior rape or two could also lead to serious, violent attacks by fellow inmates. I wanted my new client to open up to me about his history and his rape convictions without fear that others in the visiting room might hear. I imagined that he had told others he was in for murder, since his sentence was twenty-five-to-life.

Tuggle appeared in the window. He was handcuffed in front of his body; the handcuffs attached to a chain around his waist. He looked down after a quick glance at me, then watched the guard struggle to find the key to the little room. It must not have gotten used much.

Honestly, I was surprised that Tuggle was white. I didn't have all the previous records from the case, but I knew that Tuggle had two prior convictions. His most recent conviction for possession of methamphetamine landed him in prison for twenty-five-years-to-life under the three-strikes law. I guess the meth conviction should have been a clue: it was rampant in California, especially the Central Valley and other poor, white areas.

But I also knew that people of color accounted for about 60 percent of people in prison. The numbers are worse for three-strikers. According to the prison system itself, 71.2 percent of the state's three-strike population was black or Latino as of 2011. One in three African American men can expect to go to prison in their lifetime, compared to about one in seventeen white men.

Here stood that one in seventeen, framed by the wire mesh window, looking like a truck driver with no big rig or a cowboy without his horse. Tuggle's gray hair grew long over his ears and complemented a well-groomed, almost-handlebar mustache. He was tall, well over six feet. When the guard finally opened the door and Tuggle came in, I stood up, and he looked down at me.

"Just give me a wave if you have a problem," the guard said. Then he shut the door behind him—and locked it.

I felt a quick rush of fear. I was locked in a tiny room, backed into the corner, with a convicted rapist who was 6'4" and weighed 220 pounds. I stood a bit straighter, trying to look bigger than my 130 pounds.

Tuggle extended his hand; it was stopped suddenly by the chains only a few inches from his body. "Good morning, ma'am."

And suddenly, it was just so awkward. I was thirty-four. David Tuggle was old enough to be my father. He had been waiting for the Ninth Circuit to appoint him an attorney to attack the three-strikes law. I imagine that when he received the news that it had finally happened, he'd been elated. Prisoners mark even the tiniest of victories. Then I showed up—young-ish, skinny, and just passed the California Bar.

Plus, I must have looked nervous. I had handled appeals for several other clients in prison, but we'd communicated by mail. I had been in many prisons before as a student or with a senior lawyer, but this was the first time, as a lawyer, that I'd met my own client alone. I looked nervous because I *was* nervous.

But the tall man before me spoke softly and courteously. He seemed old, almost shy.

"I would really like to help. Can you begin by telling me about the day of your arrest?"

"I was driving a hot-rod van. You know, nice paint job, big tires, well-kept. It got the cops' attention. Speeding ticket. But you listen to the tapes and you'll hear them say there's a '290' up ahead."

Penal Code 290 denotes a registered sex offender. Mr. Tuggle was suggesting the police officers had recognized his license plate and were suspicious.

"But there's fifteen minutes of that tape missing. The court said they needed to have it as evidence, but the DA claimed it was lost. If we could find it, that'd show I wasn't speeding. They should have never pulled me over in the first place."

"Let's move to some of the other claims in your habeas petition. There are sixteen. Honestly, Mr. Tuggle, that seems like too many."

I urged him to narrow it down to only the claims that the court had expressed some interest in, like claim 15, that the three-strikes sentence was unconstitutional because it was not proportional to the crime and, more importantly, because the prior strikes were based on crimes that Mr. Tuggle did not commit.

Innocence is tricky. People always ask me, "Doesn't everyone say he's innocent?" or "Don't you get sick of your clients saying they didn't do it?" Most of my clients don't talk about innocence. Rather, they make legal claims: "That piece of evidence shouldn't have been allowed." "That juror shouldn't have been excused." "The police searched me or my property without good enough reason." Most legal claims have nothing to do with innocence. To me, and to the United States Constitution, those claims are just as important, if not more so. Of course innocence matters—but it's equally important for the courts to follow the rules, for juries to make decisions based on evidence, not emotion, and for judges to impose fair, reasonable sentences. These rules protect all of us.

As impossible as it might seem, every one of us stands the chance of getting entangled in the system. Every one of us wants those rules followed. We should pray at night for fairness, because innocence might not be that clear cut.

| | | | |

"Did you know?" I asked Doug, steam from the hot tub rising around us.

He had gotten the subpoena just after two o'clock that afternoon. We had spent the rest of the day calling around for lawyers, pacing, faking normalcy as we fed the kids something frozen from Trader Joe's, skipped baths, and shoved them into bed. Finally, we'd made our way out to the patio and collapsed into the steaming water.

"What do you mean?" he asked.

"Did you know what Lance was doing?"

"I don't know."

This was not the answer I expected. Of course my husband was innocent. He was 100 percent innocent. How could he not know if he was innocent or guilty?

"It's not that simple," he said. "I knew he was shady. He was always trying to get more money out of us."

I did know that. I knew that the minute Lance walked into my backyard, late, with his slicked back hair and the quick way he spoke while looking around at who else was at the party.

"He would always say the price of the house turned out to be higher than we expected, and we were always negotiating his fee. Other guys from the courthouse steps told us we couldn't trust him. They said Lance was trying to screw us and we should hire them."

"So, you suspected he was breaking the law?"

"No, not really. The others were just as bad as Lance. We thought they were saying stuff just to get our business. All of them were working together. They'd been doing it that way for years."

I envisioned five or six white guys in their thirties and forties, huddled outside of the courthouse every auction day. Instead of dark suits, they wore fancy designer jeans with bedazzled pockets hanging low on their rear-ends. Flashy watches peeked out from under the contrasting fabric cuffs of their untucked paisley button-down shirts.

"Three G's for you for the Forest Glenn house. Two for Danny for the Edgebrook condo."

Doug didn't fit into that world. My husband is a good Catholic who went to parochial schools. He raised money for Big Brothers Big Sisters when he was still in college. His company partners with organizations to provide affordable homes to people. He makes his famous Tahoe pancakes on the weekend and coaches Zach's baseball team with a patience for six-year-old boys that only a truly kind person could muster.

"Babe. If you had any inkling this was shady, you should've gotten out."

Spoken like a true lawyer. Follow the rules at all costs! Don't do anything wrong! I had lived by these mottos since childhood. I got straight A's without my mom ever having to ask if my homework was done. I had some fun as a teenager, got into mild trouble, but essentially, I was a pleaser. As an adult with three kids, a house, and a law degree, I had never been better at following rules. There was just too much to lose. But for Doug, it wasn't that simple.

"We were trying to get into the business back then. We were working our asses off, but there was no way in without these guys.

They ruled the steps. You know that. We couldn't buy foreclosures without them."

I let my hands float on the surface of the warm water but felt anger. "You put all of this, our whole family on the line so you could grow your business?" The white stucco of our pretty house glowed in the moonlight. Inside, our three kids were asleep in their beds. "All of it?"

The heat was too much; the jets seemed so loud. We had been through so much, all of the stress of the NFL, game-winning and game-losing kicks, all of the lonely wandering around the country from team to team.

"This is what you do. You take unreasonable risks."

His head bowed. Small explosions of wet heat hit his wide jaw and mouth. He dragged his hands down his face.

"You are the king of high risk and high reward."

He didn't say anything.

"And sometimes the cost is high."

| | | | |

Twenty-five-years-to-life was the cost of Tuggle's mistakes. And even though he talked about innocence, I wanted to focus on the legal claim that would win the appeal. Winning an appeal is a treacherously long road; Tuggle's roadblocks were two rape convictions.

In 1985, he picked up Debra R. hitchhiking out on Yosemite Avenue in Manteca. I knew Manteca. We went there often as kids to spend scorching Valley days at their famous waterslides. It was a working-class town, with a sugar-beet factory that made us call it "Man-stinka."

When Tuggle saw Debra on the side of the road, he quickly pulled over his four-door, yellow Datsun station wagon. He asked if she needed a ride, and she said she sure did, bending down to see him through the passenger side window.

"I'm going to Tracy," she said. "Near Grant Line Road."

"Hop in," he said. "Mind if we stop at the Moss Dale Marina up here?"

Tuggle had already had a couple beers but wanted another. After entering and exiting the mini-mart, he handed the six-pack across the middle console as he got back in the car.

"Want one?"

She did.

Tuggle drove the back way from Manteca to Tracy along the river. It was a warm evening, and the moon shone on the open fields. He pulled over near the river. They talked, drank the beers, shared a joint. They started kissing, and—with music playing on the tape deck—had sex on the hood of the yellow wagon.

Back on the road, Debra asked Tuggle if he minded stopping in at a roadside Circle K.

"No problem."

He bought some orange juice; she bought gum. He dropped her off at a corner when she asked, though it seemed like the middle of nowhere. He watched her walk through a field, jump over a fence, and disappear. He looked at the matchbook she had given him. It had two phone numbers written on it. He thought he'd give her a call the next day.

She called the police that night to report a rape.

"Did she testify at the trial?" I asked Tuggle. I was definitely interested in her side of this story. "What did she say for herself?"

"She admitted that she didn't tell me to stop. She never said no. She didn't have any injuries or bruises."

"Then what? How did she explain it?"

"She said she was scared."

"What about going to Circle K, casually asking you to stop for some gum?"

"She admitted that, too."

"What about the matchbook? How could she possibly explain why she gave you her phone number?"

"She didn't. The matchbook was off limits. The police found it when they searched my stuff, but my attorney never hired a handwriting expert to show that it was her writing. The judge just said the whole thing was irrelevant."

"Do we know why?" I asked. "I mean, did you ever figure out why she accused you?"

"She had this boyfriend." He shook his head and looked down at the table. "The guy'd had a vasectomy. His name was Raymond. I swear to God, I will never forget that. Debra told her sister around the time of all of this that she thought she was pregnant. We had evidence that she visited a gynecologist about a month after we, you know." He shifted in his chair, embarrassed. "This is hard for me. Even after all these years. I've thought about that night so many times. Replayed it over and over. Could I really have misjudged her so bad? I don't know, but I don't think so. There was a hearing and everything. About whether we could bring up her past romantic life."

"What happened with this theory about the boyfriend?"

"Oh yeah, well, my attorney tried to argue that she made up the rape to cover-up a different night with another guy, someone other than Raymond. Judge just wouldn't let it in."

"Okay. All right. What about the other conviction?"

"Her name was Nicole. Never seen her before in my life. I guess after they arrested me for the thing with Debra, they called in Nicole because her rape hadn't been solved. Happened like a year before. They showed her a photo line-up. She couldn't pick a soul. Then they had a real lineup, physical, you know. All of us standing there on the wall with stripes."

"Sure. Yes."

"Still couldn't ID anyone. She said three of the six guys looked familiar. She ended up picking some other guy—in the number-three position."

"Not you," I confirmed.

"No. Some other guy. Then this detective tells her the selection was wrong. Said something about, 'It wasn't number three, it was number four. We just arrested him for some other rape case, and we think he was the guy that raped you, too.'"

"And you were number four."

"I sure was."

"That doesn't seem like enough for a conviction."

"No kidding. They tried the rapes together. The two of them. The DA kept harping on how both happened on the outskirts of Manteca. And the car. Nicole told the police her guy drove a brown two-door hatchback. Then the police show her a picture of my car, a yellow wagon. They just made her believe the two were the same car. She just up and changed her story, said the car of the guy who raped her looked like my car."

"No DNA evidence?"

"Must've been before all that DNA stuff. Some expert did say my blood type was not inconsistent with the rape kit. But I guess the results were inconclusive. No one could be eliminated." Tuggle had become quite a good jailhouse lawyer.

"Do you know if that rape kit is still around?"

"I've written so many letters. To the lawyers, the Innocence Project, every-damn-body. Never heard a word."

| | |.| |

Later that night, placing a milky sippy cup into the dishwasher, I was thinking less about Debra and more about myself.

I started going out with Brad my sophomore year in high school. I had just turned fifteen. He was older, a senior. He played

SHANTI BRIEN

football and starred on the debate team. After a couple of months, he asked if I would have sex with him. I said no; I loved him and everything, but I wasn't ready.

Then the night of the Christmas Ball arrived in all its magnificence. Maw-maw made my dress—black velvet top with puffy sleeves, a tea-length red and green plaid taffeta skirt, big black bow at my lower back. The perm in my hair needed a refresher, but I scrunched it the best I could and curled my bangs. They rose like a crown and curled perfectly over my forehead. The dance was magical.

We ended the night at Brad's friend's house. His parents weren't home. Other guys from the football and debate teams were there, drinking with their older girlfriends who also wore taffeta and velvet. I didn't know anyone very well.

After a round of quarters, Brad led me across the lawn to the dark pool house. We started making out on the bed. The plaid taffeta came off and then the black nylons. I tried to say no, but before I knew what was happening, he had a condom on, and it was over.

He drove me home in his yellow Rabbit. We drove in silence.

I didn't feel like I was raped, but I hadn't wanted it to happen. I wished I could go back and do something differently. I wished it so badly. I wished it the next morning when I woke up and remembered, and I wished it every morning after that. It wasn't quite a prayer but a deep, empty wish.

As empty as I felt, it seemed scarier to leave him. I kept going out with Brad because I thought I was supposed to. I kept having sex with him because I knew that was what he wanted. The thought of him leaving made me feel like I would shrivel up, break apart, and blow away. *Maybe, one day*—I used to think—*we would get married.*

A couple of months later, a condom broke. Brad took me to Round Table Pizza for lunch. We sat in a booth, the cheap stained-glass windows making it feel like we were at the bottom of a well tinged with red light. I couldn't eat my personal-size Hawaiian; it just wouldn't go down.

"What are we going to do?" I said.

"You can call my sister-in-law."

"That's weird. I don't even know her."

"This same thing happened to her and my brother. They got married and it all worked out."

I really didn't know what to do. I couldn't tell my mom. I never wanted to bother her with my problems; she worked so hard. I couldn't tell Brad's sister-in-law; I didn't even know her.

"At BYU, there's married housing," Brad offered. "It could be fun."

"Just take me back to school," I said.

We went back out into the vast parking lot, back to the yellow car. Sitting on that cracking black vinyl seat, I knew that if I was pregnant, I could not have the baby. A very small piece of me believed that I could have more than a baby, that I could be more than a wife and mother. I didn't want married housing at BYU. No woman on my father's side of the family had ever gone to college, but I wanted to go. I couldn't break up with Brad. But the idea of a child made me realize that I had, somewhere deep in the back of my mind, the idea of becoming a lawyer.

As a woman who had felt pressured to have sex, I would have normally said that of course Debra should be believed. It's outrageous to think a woman would lie about being raped. If anything, we keep it to ourselves, thinking we were asking for it somehow, that somehow, it's our fault.

But Tuggle had a credible explanation. It fit with the phone numbers on the matchbook and the stop at the Circle K for gum. The bottom line was that I believed him. As for Nicole, it seemed clear that he wasn't guilty. Mistaken eyewitness identifications are one of the main reasons that juries convict innocent people. Victims and witnesses very often identify the wrong person, but juries love eyewitnesses. With the two rapes tried together in front of one jury, I could easily see them convicting Tuggle of both.

For the two rapes, Tuggle was sentenced to nine years in state prison. He served those years and was released on parole in 1991. In 1992, he pled guilty to felony receipt of stolen property and served another two years. He was on parole following this second stint when he was convicted of possession of 0.11 grams of methamphetamine in 1995, during the infancy of the three-strikes law. Tuggle received twenty-five-years-to-life.

His appeals in California took about two years. In 1998, he filed a habeas petition. His appeals were over, but he had constitutional issues with his trial and other bits of evidence he wanted a court to consider. The habeas petition was dismissed in mid-2000. He then moved to the federal courts. In September of 2000, he filed a habeas petition with the district court—the lowest of the federal courts. Almost exactly five years later, the district court judge denied Tuggle's claims. Nevertheless, after another request and another year of waiting, the court granted Tuggle the right to appeal his habeas case to the Ninth Circuit—the highest federal court before the US Supreme Court. The appeal would be limited, however, to a challenge of the three-strikes law as cruel and unusual under the Eighth Amendment. In 2007, twelve years after his conviction and ten years after he had last met with an attorney, Tuggle had me.

This was one of my first appeals in the Ninth. The three-strikes law just seemed wrong to me; people who had already served their sentences were going away to prison for life for minor offenses. Tuggle's life in prison for having 0.11 grams of meth—just one dose—seemed cruel.

Although the Eighth Amendment to the Constitution prohibits "cruel and unusual punishment"—no cutting off hands or poking out eyes—the Supreme Court has also interpreted the Eighth Amendment to forbid extreme sentences that are grossly disproportionate to the crime. But they really mean it when they say "extreme."

In 1980, William James Rummel came before the Supreme Court. His first felony conviction was fraudulent use of a credit card to obtain $80; he was then convicted of passing a forged check in the amount of $28.36; finally, Rummel committed his third felony—obtaining $120.75 by fraud. Because he had not "learned his lesson," he was sentenced to twelve-years-to-life. He would be up for parole in twelve, but parole "is an act of executive grace," according to the Supreme Court, and grace is hard to come by in Texas. Unfortunately, Mr. Rummel lived in Texas. The Supreme Court found this sentencing—for a crime amounting to several hundred dollars gained by non-violent means—perfectly acceptable.

The Supreme Court did take pity on Jerry Helm. South Dakota put him in prison for life without the possibility of parole for "uttering a 'no-account' check for $100." A bounced check. Life in prison, the Supreme Court decided in *Solem v. Helm* in 1983, just didn't seem "proportionate" to bouncing a check.

In 2003, California's three-strikes law finally made its way up to the Supreme Court. The Court found it perfectly reasonable that Leandro Andrade, an admitted heroin addict, should spend fifty-years-to-life in prison for stealing a total of $153 worth of videotapes from two different Kmart department stores.

Like most people, I have my own strikes. I could sift through my childhood and find myself copying an answer on a history test, taking money from my mom's wallet without asking, eating half my uncle's birthday cake right before his party, smoking cigarettes with friends in seventh grade then lying to my mom that "we burnt some toast. Real bad." But I also committed actual crimes, arguably worse than Rummel and Andrade. I'd shoplifted clothing at the mall. I'd driven my car after too many glasses of chardonnay. I had defrauded the DMV and/or committed identity theft (I might have been convicted of either) when I had a fake ID in college. I had most definitely, like Rummel and Helms, bounced a check or two.

The fact was, I had the good luck to not get caught. But even if I had been caught, I was clearly not the intended target of the three-strikes law. When I was seven, my mom got remarried to an emergency room nurse, and we moved to a middle-class neighborhood. He worked nights and made pretty good money. My mom had two jobs, teaching at the junior college and working at the recreation department. We didn't have fancy cars or go on vacations aside from camping, but my friends' parents were doctors and lawyers. We all had swimming pools and went to good public schools. Maw-maw was an Indian and Hal wore his hair long and carried feathers and flutes, but I basically grew up white. I was a cheerleader and an honor roll student. Pretty, middle-class cheerleaders don't "strike out."

I had a decent argument for Tuggle. The Ninth Circuit had actually shown some mercy on a couple of three-strikes defendants. One was Santos Reyes, sentenced to twenty-five-years-to-life for committing perjury through misrepresenting information on a DMV application—not unlike my fake ID. Tuggle also had a very minor triggering crime, and although rape is a serious offense, I was working on proving he hadn't raped those women.

Tuggle's third strike was possession of 0.11 grams of methamphetamine—again, about one dose. The law considers possession of that amount of the drug a "wobbler"—it could be charged as a felony or a misdemeanor, whichever the district attorney decides. With no prior convictions, Tuggle would have likely been charged with a misdemeanor and received probation. The DA in *People v. Tuggle* must have been in a really bad mood. Or else he was looking for a promotion. DAs are driven by conviction statistics and often seem to view life sentences like notches on their belts. The three-strikes law was brand new in 1995, and DAs across the state were trying to see how far they could push it.

In my written arguments, I told the Ninth Circuit that Tuggle's case pushed it too far. His triggering crime was almost like bouncing a check, a stupid mistake that hurt no one but himself. Sure, he had a criminal past, but the trend was decreasing violence. And, he was wrongly convicted.

I could not have been more nervous as I entered the Ninth Circuit courthouse to present and defend my arguments. The courtroom seemed designed to instill fear in young lawyers, with heavy, dark, wooden benches like church pews, white marble columns, and huge gothic arched windows. Sun beat down through the windows, cooking through my black jacket. Because our case was third or fourth on the calendar, I waited over two hours for the clerk to call us. Sweat soaked through my suit jacket and formed dark circles under my armpits.

Before the proceedings began, a deputy attorney general, an employee of California charged with defending the state's convictions, sauntered over to introduce himself. He had a full head of dark hair, navy suit, red tie. He looked twenty-two years old. His voice carried so much young-guy swagger that I had trouble remembering the name he gave. *Justin something?* I don't know how he knew I represented Tuggle; maybe it was the sweaty pits.

"Do you happen to have an extra copy of your reply brief?" he asked.

It must have taken me a few seconds to pick my jaw up from the ground, because before I could answer, he said, "Oh, it's cool. No problem. I didn't get a chance to read it. My secretary must have misplaced it. It's not really necessary."

I had spent 24.8 hours writing that reply brief. I had responded point-by-point to the arguments this guy had put forth. The document now included the declaration from the Innocence Project attorney. I had asked that the case be remanded (sent back to the lower court) until the DNA got retested. Young Justin hadn't even read it? I was so busy being horrified that I was surprised when our case was called.

I approached the podium. The combined age of the three judges looming above me was over 200. Together, they had well over 100 years of legal experience. Their black robes matched expressions of dark boredom.

I took a deep breath and said: "This court has been known to say that the State of California's sentencing policy under the three-strikes-law is not only inhumane but misguided. Nowhere is the truth of that more evident than in this case. David Tuggle was sentenced to twenty-five-years-to-life for possession of one dose of methamphetamine. The prior strikes used to enhance that sentence are now deeply in question."

I spoke about the principle of gross proportionality. But my argument was focused on asking the court to delay their decision so a lower court could determine if Tuggle was actually innocent of the two prior strikes.

"After all, without knowing the truth about prior convictions, how could a crime of possession of one dose of a drug rise to the level of a sentence of twenty-five-years-to-life? There is strong evidence that Mr. Tuggle is innocent," I continued, "yet we come to you acknowledging that crucial evidence has not yet been developed. We are requesting a remand so someone can give due consideration to those prior convictions."

"The problem with a rEEmand," the first judge jumped in with a deep, soft, Southern voice, "is for how many years would the rEEmand be if you rEEmanded it?"

"I couldn't say . . . for certain . . . at this moment. I would need—"

"You couldn't even predict, based on this recAArd, based on this conviction and based on what's there. Could you?"

I didn't like where this was going. The judge was African American, born in Alabama, and appointed by Jimmy Carter. I had hoped for some support, some easy questions.

"I do know that the Northern California Innocence Project is diligently pursuing the claim," I responded. "I do know that Mr. Tuggle has spent quite a number of years in prison, perhaps unlawfully and unconstitutionally, and he would love for the claims to be pursued as quickly as possible."

"Well, *Andrade* and that line of cases poses a problem for you." Judge Two's voice was breathy, like a sigh. I sensed regret. He was a Montana man with a graying, nicely trimmed beard. I imagined he and David Tuggle would be outdoorsy pals under different circumstances. But this judge was known for his evenhandedness; he was just going to apply the law.

Still, I tried to make the best of those cases that Judge Two thought were bad for me. "In those cases, and others, the Supreme Court has stated that we must look at the factual circumstances of the underlying crime. And that is what we are requesting. That this court allow the district court or the state court to do so. And that line of Supreme Court precedent goes all the way back to *Solem v. Helm.*"

I mentioned the case where the life sentence for a bounced check was overturned because, one, it was a great case with an exceedingly minor triggering crime that got resolved in the defendant's favor; and two, Judge Number Three, the ancient South Dakotan directly in front of me, had written the decision in *Solem v. Helm* as a judge in the Eighth Circuit. The Supreme Court liked his decision, and I liked it, too. Judge Three took my bait.

"I know that case," he shouted.

He'd been leaning back in his black leather chair, but came well forward now. Judge Three had been appointed to the federal bench by Lyndon Johnson. He had heard almost 6,000 cases. It took a lot to get his attention.

"[Your Honor] authored that opinion in 1983 with great foresight into upcoming Eighth Amendment jurisprudence," I told the court. "He looked at Helm's sentence and said, 'Wait a minute. Isn't it the true facts of Helm's underlying crimes that make this different, that make this sentence unconstitutional?' The Supreme Court obviously agreed and upheld the decision."

I was clearly trying to win points with the man, but I had no shame. I wanted him to remember the feeling of doing the right thing—even if it was not the easy thing—then having the Supreme Court say, "Good job, Judge."

I closed by asking the court to remand, to send the case back down to other courts to determine the validity of the facts underpinning Tuggle's rape convictions.

"Please do not allow this inhumane and misguided law to trump constitutional rights or to trump justice for Mr. Tuggle." I waited a beat, looking directly at the judges, then turned and took my seat, exhausted but exhilarated.

In his navy suit and too-bright tie, young Justin stepped to the podium. "This is an Eighth Amendment case. And when a reviewing court looks at an Eighth Amendment claim, they are not worried about whether the underlying convictions are valid."

Judge Three said, "You have three-strikes, and you're out. If one of those strikes is not a strike, if it's a ball, then three-strikes shouldn't apply. Isn't that true?"

"That's absolutely true, Your Honor."

"I realize this is a habeas case," the judge continued. "I realize also that at the state sentencing you could . . . show that the prior convictions are invalid. But very often there is not the ability to do that at the time. So, I don't really see why this is such a horrendous request."

"Mr. Tuggle had his day in court. He had a trial. He had an attorney. He had a jury. The jury returned a verdict of guilty on all of his convictions. He went from there to the California Court of Appeal. He had his day in court there, where he had a chance to invalidate his convictions." Justin continued on and on about all the judges who had upheld Tuggle's convictions.

I wanted to stand up and blurt out that the DNA had never been retested! That the matchbook phone numbers needed to be considered! But from the way the discussion proceeded, the judges seemed to be considering my argument. Judge Two had the most reservations about reconsidering the prior convictions. He seemed to feel bound to preserve those convictions, as the judges before him had. Judges inhabit a special, elite group who vigilantly defend one another.

With that, Judge Two said, "This is an interesting case. Thank you for your arguments."

The three judges would consider our positions and appoint one of them to write a decision. We wouldn't know the outcome for months.

When the only people left were the young law clerks, the judges, the Justin guy and me, the room seemed to relax some.

"Judge [Three]," said Judge [Two], "this is our last day with you. I want to thank you again for coming down. And I want to thank my dear friend, Judge [One]. It's always such a pleasure to sit with you. I argued my first case in front of Judge [One] here in the Ninth Circuit."

"Oh," he said in his deep, smoky voice, "that just shows how old I am."

The law clerks laughed.

"*Always* a pleasure when there's twenty-five inches of snow in Fargo," Judge Three said.

The thin crowd laughed; every one of them seemed thankful that talk of weather meant no more thoughts of innocent people in prison for life for one dose of meth.

Despite my hours of preparation, my meticulous research, the hours away from my kids, and my sincere belief that Tuggle had a chance, I realized Assistant US Attorney Justin did not even need to glance at my briefs for one simple reason: I represented a convicted rapist who was caught breaking the law again. This was not stolen VCR tapes from Kmart or bouncing a check—this was really bad stuff. The job of appellate judges is to find a way to uphold the decision of the court below it. Justin What's-His-Face knew how slim my chances were.

On some level, maybe I did, too. Maybe my hope was child-ish and naïve. There was nothing I could say, there was no level of ambivalence or laziness that this someday-politician wise-guy Justin could have that would cause him to lose this case. If the courts overturned many cases, we'd have chaos and anarchy; the system would grind to a stop. I had no doubt that without DNA evidence showing that Tuggle didn't commit the rapes, the judges had plenty to uphold his three-strike sentence. Justin had won the case before we had even started.

A few months later, he officially won. I was disappointed. Yet, I had done everything I could. I had presented the best possible arguments to the Ninth Circuit. I told Tuggle's true story to three very intelligent, influential people. They heard about the pri-or rapes and the evidence that might show his innocence. They listened when I told them about the absurdity of imprisoning someone for life for having one dose of a drug in the pocket of his jeans. They had really listened. Maybe they didn't agree. Or maybe they did, but felt bound to follow their interpretation of Supreme Court precedent. Either way, Tuggle had gotten his day in court.

Plus, we still had the Innocence Project.

5

CHAPTER 3

🔑

THE WAR ON DRUGS

When the Ninth Circuit appointed me to represent Fetu Faraimo, I knew we would lose. From the records I received—a few faded copies of court docket sheets and denials of many appeals and even more habeas petitions—I could not have realized that saving the life of this forty-something Samoan father-of-four would be my greatest legal accomplishment.

The story of how Faraimo and his family became victims of the War on Drugs began when Guam customs agents intercepted an express mail package containing more than 200 grams of methamphetamine. The package was addressed to a Tom Smith at a postal box in a private mail service store in a run-down strip mall. American and Guam customs agents decided to stage a sting by removing most of the methamphetamine, replacing the drugs with pseudomethamphetamine, and waiting. Finally, the officers saw Smith retrieve the package from the postal facility and depart in a Toyota pickup. His friend Faraimo was waiting in the passenger seat.

Officers followed some distance behind the truck. They were led into a remote area of Guam, where a house sat at the end of a dirt road. They surrounded the house with guns drawn and approached the front door. Smith answered and led them inside. Searching the house, they found a locked bedroom.

"US Customs! Open this goddamn door!"

Fetu Faraimo threw the door open and jumped back. In his hand was a small kitchen knife. His wife and children huddled behind his large Samoan body. The room was a mess—bedding and clothes scattered everywhere, remnants of the parcel's packaging lying in plain view.

Arrested and handcuffed, Faraimo pleaded, "Please keep my family out of this."

In exchange for the authorities leaving his wife and children alone, Faraimo admitted that the package was his and that he'd received other packages of meth from California. Faraimo then led the agents around the property, showing them where he'd buried prior drug shipments.

This would be his last night with his family in Guam.

In 1997, a jury found Faraimo guilty of three counts of importation of methamphetamine from California and three counts of possession with intent to distribute drugs. At sentencing for those convictions, Faraimo faced mandatory minimum sentences, the policy equivalent of a death spiral leading to a super massive black hole.

It wasn't too long ago that mandatory minimums became a thing. In 1951, Congress enacted a mandatory minimum penalty of two years of imprisonment for violating the Narcotic Drugs Import and Export Act, which broadly prohibited the importation, sale, purchase, and receipt of controlled substances.[1] In 1986, at the height of the crack cocaine "epidemic," Congress doubled down on mandatory minimums. "The Kingpins" and "The Masterminds"—identified by the amount of drugs with which they were involved—would now get ten years in prison *for their first convictions.*[2] Only two years later, mandatory minimums for involvement in a drug enterprise increased yet again to ten-to-twenty.[3]

We get numb to these numbers, just as Congress has, but if you think about spending one *month* in prison—the absolute loss of freedom and home and anything resembling comfort—and the ridiculous fear that would engender, the idea of one year or ten years or twenty years *for your first offense* becomes all the more stark.

In 1998, Justice Stephen Breyer of the United States Supreme Court disparaged mandatory minimum sentences in a very diplomatic and restrained way: "By 1991, Congress had created nearly 100 separate mandatory minimum provisions, located in about 60 different criminal statutes, including gun and drug statutes . . . But it is difficult to find good reasons for that popularity." Even the US Sentencing Commission, the body tasked with developing and recommending sentences for federal crimes, strongly opposed mandatory minimums from the beginning.

Still, Faraimo, quite possibly the antithesis of a "Mastermind," felt the brunt of this contested, uncertain, unwise mechanism for sentencing. Based on his two prior felony drug convictions and the large weight of the drugs that he'd voluntarily surrendered from the packages scattered throughout his property, Faraimo received

---

1 Report to Congress: Mandatory Minimums in the Federal Criminal Justice System (Oct, 2011) at 22.

2 Report to Congress: Mandatory Minimums in the Federal Criminal Justice System (Oct, 2011) at 24, quoting Senate Minority leader Robert Byrd.

3 Id.

four life sentences plus a thirty-year sentence to run concurrently. Four life sentences. *Plus* thirty years. He was shipped to a federal prison on the mainland, 6,000 miles away.

Faraimo found me after ten years of appeals and handwritten habeas petitions. He started with a direct appeal to the Ninth Circuit to overrule prior cases that held that one could be convicted of "importing" drugs into Guam (a territory of the United States) from other states. Faraimo argued that since one could not "import" drugs from one state of the United States to another, and since Guam was equivalent to a state, you could not technically import drugs into Guam from California. Another federal court of appeals had agreed with that argument and reversed a conviction in another case pertaining to importation of drugs into Guam.

There are twelve courts of appeals in the federal court system, each one of them representing a large region or circuit, and a thirteenth court representing Washington, D.C. These courts are only required to follow what the US Supreme Court says and prior decisions their circuit has made. The Ninth Circuit ignored the other court's opinion; they simply left the question of importation out of their decision to deny Faraimo's appeal. His attorney didn't pursue it.

Faraimo was appointed another attorney for the appeal of his habeas petition. She failed to raise the importation issue at all, though she raised it for another client, Roy Cabacaang, in the same situation at virtually the same time.

In Cabacaang's case, six years after Faraimo was convicted but during the time his habeas petition was pending, the Ninth Circuit abruptly overruled itself and held that transit of drugs directly from California to Guam did *not* constitute "importation." Three of Faraimo's crimes were no longer crimes. It sounds simple: notify the court that the crimes aren't crimes, get them stricken from the records, and get a judge to reconsider the sentence.

Not. Even. Close.

On his own, Faraimo had spent seven years going from court to court, asserting that his crimes were no longer crimes because of *Cabacaang*. Each court denied him because he should have raised the issue earlier—during his direct appeal, for example—or in a different court, like the one where he'd been convicted, not where he was imprisoned. He then tried all of those; each answered with a different nuance, but they all essentially said they simply did not care that his convictions were for crimes that no longer existed. There was a large amount of drugs involved, and he had admitted to police that they were his. Of course, they used legal terms like "actual innocence," "unobstructed procedural opportunities to present the claim," and "escape hatch" to a Section 2255 petition. But in the end, the decision was the same. Faraimo was in prison for four life sentences plus thirty years. This was the 1990s, after all. President Bush's War on Drugs was raging, and the government didn't give a second thought to enemy bodies rotting on the battlefield.

| | | | |

I was once almost taken as the enemy.

I was an exchange student in Costa Rica, a junior in high school, when a black-haired man in a dark suit approached the small group of us standing in the tiny private-plane airport. "Perdóname."

Ricardo, the Costa Rican I had been dating, started talking rapidly in Spanish with the man. I had been in the country for over six months, and although my Spanish had gotten very good, I could only make out "Puerto Limón" (the city on the eastern shore where we were heading) and "inmigración." My American friend, Adria, and I only glanced at each other, accustomed to missing most of what was being said around us. As two or three other dark suits approached, Ricardo turned away, covered his mouth, and started coughing loudly.

The man escorted us out of the lobby. The lobby was the entire airport. In the corner, an espresso machine sat on a rickety wood cart with a tower of chips and a few stale pastries under plastic beside two small tables. A single man sitting at a desk seemed to run the entire aviation department, including air traffic control. There was no one else in the building to do it.

Out of the lobby and into a small room, that man patted Ricardo down.

"Where are you from?" he asked me in Spanish.

"The United States," I answered in his language, feeling grateful for my new skills.

"What are you doing in the airport?"

"We are taking my friend, here, to Puerto Limón for the weekend."

Adria was almost six feet tall with blonde hair down her back. She had an invitation to spend the weekend on the Caribbean side of the country. She was sixteen, like me, but her host mom didn't care what she did. Ricardo's father had an airplane. Ricardo was only nineteen, but told us he was a good pilot; incredibly, I thought it was a great idea to fly with him across the country.

"Passports?" the officer asked me and Adria.

She handed hers over.

"I'm sorry. I don't have it with me," I said.

"Where it is?" the officer asked, impatience and mistrust in his voice.

"It's at my host family's house. Not far from here."

My host family lived in an upper-middle-class neighborhood in the capital. Rocío, the mom, doted on her three children, two in high school and one persistent, annoying seven-year-old. Her curly black hair bounced around as she called them to dinner and danced to the Gypsy Kings. The father, Javier, worked for an American pharmaceutical company. He spoke good English and helped me through the first really hard weeks. They were wonderful, and I didn't want them involved, but I had no choice. I gave the officer the name of my family and the phone number of the house.

Then, Ricardo, Adria, and I were alone in the small room. Ricardo was strikingly handsome; his dark hair slightly long and wavy, eyes dark, and jawline strong. Adria had met him first and was jealous that he took me to bars and parties.

"What's going on?" I asked.

His English was great. We never spoke Spanish.

"They want your passports."

"I got that part. Is this just some immigration thing, like they think we're here illegally?"

"Not exactly."

"Are they letting us go to Puerto Limón?" Adria asked.

"They might. But not without your passport." He looked at me.

We waited for hours. I called home, hoping someone would bring my passport. Abuelita, Rocío's aging mother, was the only one there. She scurried around, cooking and cleaning all day, but could not find it. The agents wouldn't let me leave. When Rocío got home, the officers arranged a call.

"I'm sending a cab," Rocío told me. "I'll send your passport with it so they can identify you, but you get in the cab and come home immediately. The police think your friend is smuggling drugs."

"What are you talking about?"

"Ricardo. They think he's heavily involved in drugs, selling them, exporting them."

"Oh my God."

"¡Venga a casa! ¡Ya!"

When Rocío actually yelled, ordering me home, I knew how mad she was. Thoughtful and trusting, she'd thought I was hanging out with Adria downtown, maybe shopping for the bracelets we had stacked up to our elbows.

When my passport arrived, they let the three of us go. We walked out into the small parking lot surrounded by the dense green tick and swish of jungle. Ricardo whispered to me that he did have some cocaine, but not a lot. He'd swallowed it when we were first approached. I stared at him; his eyes suddenly seemed too dark and hollow. I collapsed into the cab and vowed never to see Ricardo again.

My host family grounded me for a month—the rest of my stay. I didn't complain. I couldn't believe how stupid I had been. I could have been arrested, convicted of being some kind of accomplice. I could have died in the plane, with Ricardo the pilot high on cocaine.

I missed home desperately, even more than I had when I'd first arrived. Part of me had run away from Brad and memories of that winter formal. He smothered me, but I missed him. He had dropped out of BYU and was back in Modesto, waiting impatiently for me to come home.

A semester away had been too much for me and the people I'd left behind; I wondered how Faraimo's family was holding up without him, and how much longer Faraimo could wait.

In a federal prison in Southern California, facing multiple life sentences, Fetu Faraimo remained patient yet persistent. Ultimately, I wanted to get Faraimo freed from prison someday, even if he were an old man when he walked out. But first I had to convince the Ninth Circuit to listen to our argument. I tried to distill ten years of legal maneuvering into a simple two-part argument: one, the court erred by not addressing Faraimo's importation argument in his direct appeal when they simply left it out of their opinion; two, his attorney provided ineffective assistance of counsel (a remarkable oversight), as she'd failed to raise the issue in his habeas appeal even though she had raised the exact issue for another client. Both of these options had flaws. As a fallback argument, I said it was a manifest injustice to leave convictions in place for crimes that were no longer crimes.

With my oral argument in the Ninth Circuit approaching, I began researching the three judges that would comprise the deciding panel. By some small miracle, Betty Binns Fletcher was on the list. Appointed by President Carter in 1979 as one of the first women to the Ninth Circuit, she was known as the "Lioness of Liberalism." She was known to extol the virtues of judicial "empathy," which has become a slur in the mouths of conservatives. Faraimo needed empathy. The other judges on the panel would be a Clinton-appointee and former Legal Aid lawyer, and Judge Forman, a Reagan-appointee visiting from the East Coast. I thought the mix of roaring liberalism and buttoned-up Reaganomics could be interesting.

I flew to Pasadena for the oral argument. I felt accomplished and professional just to be on a business trip. The girls were eight and nine. Ceci was seeing a therapist about extreme tantrums—$120 per hour to teach her how to take deep breaths. Lilli had been diagnosed with a lazy eye and spent hours every day wearing a patch. At school, she and another disruptive boy had been placed in the middle of the room so as not to distract the students sitting in the circle around them. Zach, our third, was still a baby. He slept through the night, but my world was a maelstrom of poopy diapers, organic baby food, missing soccer cleats, and library books.

Desperate for a break, I happily boarded Southwest. A single, uninterrupted hour was an unimaginable luxury. I read over my notes, but I was prepared, so I sneaked an ultra-indulgent joy—forty minutes of *House Beautiful* and *Vanity Fair*.

Arriving into John Wayne airport, I caught a cab to the courthouse in Pasadena. Again, I felt like such a professional, an actual grown-up riding in a cab that I would "expense." I was, of course, wearing my black suit.

San Francisco's courthouse exudes grandeur, but the Ninth Circuit in Pasadena is California-cool, dusty pink Spanish-style stucco with a red tile roof and a large tower. Tall palm trees lean toward the building, and immaculate gardens welcome lawyers, defendants, and the ever-present smattering of protestors.

The courtroom itself had an even more laid-back feel. I wondered if my linen suit would have been more appropriate.

After a quarter-hour of nervous waiting, a rounded door swung open in the terracotta wall, and three figures entered in their long black robes. Judge Fletcher was surprisingly short. She shuffled in with a walker, white head hunched over so she looked directly down at the ground. But when she sat on the bench and put on her glasses, she grew. She was my potential ally, the "empathetic" one, but the set of her aged face was anything but soft, which made me even more nervous.

I stepped from behind the dark wooden table and up to the podium.

"May it please the court," I paused to consciously breathe, "Shanti Brien for appellant."

"What," Judge Forman didn't let me finish, "is at stake in this case? One-hundred-fifty dollars?"

"I'm ... sorry?"

"What ... is ... at ... stake ... at this stage? Was there a fifty-dollar special assessment at the time?"

I had absolutely no idea what he was talking about. "I'm ... not sure we're talking about the same case." I laughed with nervous disbelief. "Mr. Faraimo is arguing that he meets the requirements of the escape hatch of Section—"

"I understand that," Judge Forman interrupted again. "I'm just trying to understand how many times this case has gone back and forth over what appears to me to be possibly a hundred or a hundred-fifty dollars. I don't see any injustice here."

"To my client, it's about innocence. He is challenging all of his convictions and the other life sentences, but . . ."

"He's not challenging them here. He lost the other challenges. He's serving a life sentence that seems to be totally insulated from challenge at this point. And what this back and forth is all about . . . [all] I can see is one-hundred-fifty dollars in special assessments. Was it two counts of importation or three?"

"Three."

"Ok, so it was one-hundred-fifty."

I admitted that $150 was at stake, $50 for each importation conviction we were challenging. These small fines are considered "collateral consequences" of a conviction. But I pointed out to Judge Forman that the US Attorney had admitted that, even if minor, collateral consequences were enough to justify the proceedings we were now in.

Judge Forman leaned into the microphone, not yelling, but not calm, either. He explained that I was wasting his time. He said the Ninth Circuit saw Faraimo's case years before, and the denial of that appeal created the "law of the case," a law that bound him and the other two judges to deny Faraimo again.

I couldn't believe this man was wasting *my* time. We were a solid three minutes into my eight-minute argument, and I had only muttered an inappropriate laugh and something about innocence.

"The manifest injustice here," I started again, "is actual innocence. Mr. Faraimo is not guilty on those three counts."

"This is just—" the judge practically spat with frustration. "Actual innocence? Your client possessed methamphetamine. I always forget the difference between duplicitous and multiplicitous, but it's as if he were charged with five counts of doing the same thing instead of three. I mean, that's basically it. He possessed methamphetamine with the intent to distribute it. On two counts, they labeled it 'importation' instead of distribution. It's hard for me. I am very sympathetic to true innocence arguments—"

Really?! I thought.

"—but the whole procedural posture of this case seems to reflect Judge Friendly's view that if a man from Mars suddenly showed up, we would have a hard time explaining to him what was going on."

"I agree that the case is procedurally complicated and interesting," I conceded. "Two points: first, Mr. Faraimo's actual innocence of the three convictions *does* mean something. He is hopeful that—"

"Why should I care that it is important to him? He has nothing else to do but file these petitions. We go through them. I would need a chart to keep track of it all, but people in jail have nothing better to do. The basic fact is that I cannot see any injustice in this case."

"Let me," a delicate voice interrupted, "let me ask you a question."

Judge Fletcher to the rescue.

"The First Circuit changed its opinion on this rule about importation quite a few years ago," she said. "Should we say that at that point it could have been fully challenged by Mr. Faraimo?"

"No," I stated. "Absolutely not. Even after the First Circuit's decision, there were decisions coming out of this Circuit holding the opposite. It really wasn't until *Cabacaang* that the law was changed. So, this case is very much unlike *Harrison*, where the subsequent cases were more a refining or an explanation or a definition of terms. This was a complete reversal of what the case law had been." Finally, I was able to make an argument.

Judge Forman sat back from the microphone now, looking satisfied that he'd consumed over half of my time and had left only a couple of minutes for the other judges.

"I guess the issue that Judge Forman is raising," there was my champion, her voice barely audible, a little gray-haired mouse, "is that the court ruled against your client; so, should we say that the law of the case precludes a change?"

"There are several reasons why the law of the case should not apply here," I said. "One is that the [original decision] was clearly erroneous. That decision did not consider an interesting complication, which is that Mr. Faraimo actually did present his importation claim to the Ninth Circuit."

"And the first time nobody mentioned it," Judge Fletcher added.

"Everyone ignored that it happened. That is evidence that the claim was really not available at that time. That was not addressed by the Ninth Circuit," I said.

"The claim was available!" Judge Forman jumped back in. "He made [the claim]; he simply lost. What was the impediment here for him raising that argument?"

"The clearly erroneous decision of the Ninth Circuit. And a manifest injustice," I said.

"I don't see any manifest injustice here. He has a mandatory life sentence. It's troubling to read the history of this case and [all of the habeas petitions he has filed]." The judge was fuming. "This guy was dealing in methamphetamine!"

"Although I can see that you are not sympathetic to Mr. Faraimo, if we look at Cabacaang's case, the defendants were convicted of multiple counts of possession and importation. Their convictions were reversed."

I wanted to add, "They were resentenced." If Faraimo could get another sentencing hearing, with three convictions instead of six, things could be very different. But I couldn't, because Forman had interrupted again.

"I understand your point, Ms. Brien, but that was on direct appeal. I don't see any—Ha!" He actually chuckled at himself. "I am not going to say it again." But then he did: "I don't see any injustice. The injustice here is to the judicial system that has put up with repeated efforts by the defendant over what appears to be nothing." Then he made it personal: "Which includes the time *you* might better have spent representing someone who was a victim of real injustice."

I stood with one hand gripping the podium, wishing I had something at hand that I might *throw* at the man. The judge seemed to be implying that I was personally abusing the judicial system by zealously advocating for my client—a client the Ninth Circuit appointed me to represent. Hands empty, I decided to hurl words.

"I would argue, Your Honor, that there is a grave injustice here. Faraimo has a claim of actual innocence. His convictions and three life sentences are for crimes that are *no longer crimes*. My client, for some reason that I am failing to understand, cannot get the courts to address his claims, largely because the court seems to have an utter lack of sympathy for him."

"[T]his guy is not a terribly sympathetic character," Forman asserted again.

But my time had nearly run out. "In conclusion, and for these reasons, Appellant asks that the habeas petition is granted and Mr. Faraimo's convictions are overturned."

I practically fell into my seat, feeling like I'd just gone nine rounds with George Foreman, not Judge Forman. Still, I needed to pay attention to the US Attorney. Government Girl was a young prosecutor, smart looking with glasses and long black hair. I was going to have to address her arguments in my rebuttal.

She started by agreeing with Judge Forman. She listed all the appeals and habeas petitions that Faraimo had presented, almost a decade of work. Her office alone had completed three whole briefs, maybe sixty hours of work, to the Ninth Circuit. Amazingly, the audience did not gasp.

And then the Lioness of Liberalism roared, interrupting the Government Girl with "Okay, but everyone has been wrong all along the way, is that not right?"

"Uh. Well. I don't think the issue of him being legally innocent is enough at this stage."

"But he is actually innocent. He did not commit a crime for three of the convictions," Judge Fletcher stated. I wanted to take her soft, old face in both my hands and kiss her. "What if the facts were that if you took away these three crimes that the sentence for the others would be less, would your position still be the same?"

"Well. The position would be the same."

"But it would be a more difficult case," the third judge chimed in.

"It would be a more sympathetic case," the young prosecutor admitted.

I couldn't believe she conceded something.

"You know, Judge Forman raised a very good point," Judge Fletcher said, in what was likely to be the final statement. "Why waste all of this judicial time on a case like Faraimo's? If the government just said, 'Yeah, we'll wipe out those three counts,' we would have all gone home. End of the story."

Excellent point. I wished I'd thought of it.

I wished I could be that tiny, white-haired, bespectacled powerhouse. Because, just like that, it was over. In one sentence, Betty Binns Fletcher turned Judge Forman's whole argument back around at him.

He, like so many people, including a surprising number who corner me at cocktail parties, just don't understand why I "waste" my time and energy and why the government has to "waste" so many resources on people like Faraimo, criminals in federal prisons and on death row having decent, if not comfortable lives provided by the taxpayers.

But what if we thought about it in another way? Instead of criminals wasting money by constantly appealing, perhaps the government is wasting taxpayer dollars by charging people with crimes and upholding convictions instead of admitting their mistakes. The government is responsible for criminalizing more and more behaviors, for prosecuting more and more crimes, for increasing sentences so that ten years in prison is doled out as easily as a grande latte.

This was Betty Binns Fletcher's point: if the government had simply said, ten years ago, "You're right, Mr. Faraimo, those three convictions are not crimes anymore, we will strike those from your record and make sure your sentence reflects three convictions instead of six," the case would have been over in a flash. But the government fought and fought and fought. Faraimo could not write a complete sentence, and yet he took repeated legal beatings by the government of the United States and persevered.

I might actually win a resentencing, I thought as I pushed through the doors into the sunshine pouring through a vine-grown trellis.

In the cab, I let my head fall back against the seat and soaked in rolling green Pasadena hills all the way back to the airport.

Nine months and six days later, we won.

We won in a published decision, meaning the case would be printed in the legal reports and could be relied upon as "the law" for other defendants. The very best part of the decision? Betty Binns Fletcher had ordered resentencing. Another judge would take a look at Faraimo's remaining convictions and possibly reduce his sentence. This proved that Judge Forman was wrong all along—the case did mean something. Technicalities and mistakes that might amount to only $150 worth of fines in the larger justice system meant something to the individual, to Fetu Faraimo, to his wife and to his five children.

Six weeks after the decision, I walked up our leafy driveway with the mail in my hands and opened an envelope containing this:

Dear Ms. Brien:

I received your letter with the court order that was filed on may 17 2010 and I have reader your letter and understand must of it. but I must say thank you very much there is not that much thank you in this world, and would like you to know that you have done a fine job.

Anyway I just want you to no that I have learn so much from being in prison and that the crimes will not pay, because everyone will learn from they mistake, now all I do is tell people to stay away from Drug and the crimes because there are only two places that their will in up one is prison the one is 6 ft under and that not good so ever time I talk with people I tell them was I am going through it not easy when you have a family.

So I will be waiting on you responded, and I will always prayer, that one day I can be back home with my kids.

God bless you!!

F. Faraimo

I savored Mr. Faraimo's thank you. I believed that ten years in prison had taught him the disadvantages of crime. I believed that he had learned from his mistakes. But his prayer to see his children touched my mothering core. And it touched the five-year-old me sitting on that scary clown's lap. His children probably didn't even miss him anymore. They didn't know him. Because he "lived" in

Southern California—in a prison—maybe they had fantasies that he worked with dolphins. I doubted they visited him from Guam.

Secretly, while examining briefs for the Faraimo case, researching the federal sentencing guidelines, and reading the man's heartfelt letter, I started placing myself in the role of the people waiting at home, the role of the wife of a man who'd been imprisoned.

I mostly didn't believe that Doug would be locked away, but a darker side of me obsessively sharpened the vision of Doug in a dank or blazing cell block. We would definitely visit him. I could picture him wearing the chambray shirt buttoned up to the top. I could feel the cold linoleum table and the cracked fiberglass chairs of the visiting area. I could see the confusion and fear in the kids' long dark-lashed framed eyes as we approached him, their father looking paler, maybe a little gaunt. Lilli might crack a joke about his bad outfit. Ceci would want to sit on his lap—even as a ten-year-old. Doug would be smiling, of course, elated to see the kids. He would hug them ferociously and talk only about the positive: only a few months left before he got home, or how the food was not so bad, or requests to tell him all about that goal they scored.

He might feign sunniness, but I would be a wreck. Abandonment issues? Check. Pessimistic personality? Check. Worst-case-scenario lawyer training? Check. Highly reinforced doubt about the reasonableness of prosecutors? Check. Deep, deep love and respect for my hard-working and extraordinary husband? Definitely.

As I braced for a long legal battle for Doug, possibly prison time, and the emotional havoc it would create for my marriage and family, I had no idea of the legal chaos about to hit me and Fetu Faraimo.

CHAPTER 4

DOUBLE JEOPARDY

I never met Deandra Jones (we only communicated by mail), but I connected with her instantly. She seemed like a typical mom with two kids. Her girls were ages four and seven; I had two girls of my own, just a bit older. Deandra's girls had different fathers, just like my sister and me. One of the fathers lived in Kentucky. *He must never see his girl*, I thought, *just like my father, off somewhere in Southern California when I was young.* Deandra was raising her kids in Sacramento, a Central Valley town not unlike the Modesto I grew up in. Deandra had worked for over two years in the accounts receivable department of a company. She was a young African American woman with a decent, steady job. She had been arrested once over a fight at a party, but nothing had come of it. Until the day she was arrested for a violent armed robbery, Deandra had a clean record. Like her trial attorney said, she seemed like a regular middle-class girl. Just like me, except for one night.

Frost had collected around the edges of the windows of the video store. Christmas carols played over the store's speakers as the

Wangs walked in. They lingered in the new releases aisle; married for so long, they kept bickering about which movie to pick.

"Get down!" Two dark figures yelled as they crashed open the glass doors. They both wore gloves and had guns in their hands. One sounded like a woman.

"Open the safe and the registers," the male said to the cashier, his gun trained on her.

"The safe's got a . . . a . . . delay. I'll open this register."

At the male's back, the female was yelling, "I have a gun. Armed robbery! Get to the floor!"

The Wangs stared as she walked quickly down an aisle toward them. As the woman pushed Mrs. Wang to the floor, Mrs. Wang noticed her green backpack.

"Get on the floor!" she screamed at Mr. Wang, who had started to run away but tripped. He lay still on the floor.

The shiny gold scarf wound around the robber's face left only her eyes and the bridge of her nose exposed; she stared at Mr. Wang on the floor, giving Mrs. Wang time to notice her blue jeans, blue hooded sweatshirt, and the distinctive gold headscarf. The robber, according to a frightened Mrs. Wang, was a light-skinned black woman. As she moved away from where Mrs. Wang laid in the aisle, she seemed to walk on her toes, her heels never touching the ground.

After five or ten seconds of praying that the shooter not kill her husband, Mrs. Wang rose from her belly and crept down another aisle. The female robber rushed to her.

"I told you get down!"

Mrs. Wang looked at the woman's face, still covered by the scarf. Mrs. Wang saw the woman's eyes and bridge of her nose before she grabbed Mrs. Wang's hair and pushed her to the floor again. After the woman walked away, Mrs. Wang slowly got to her knees. She crawled along the racks of videos and climbed under a table. The robbers took about $500 and ran out the way they had come in.

The employee called 9-1-1. To police, she described the robbers as "Asian" or "dark Asian" and stated that "they weren't dark-complected black; they were light-complected black if they were black."

Rahul Patel happened to be in his car outside the video store. When he saw masked people in dark clothing run inside, he called 9-1-1 to report a robbery. As he tried to drive away, a gold Infiniti blocked the exit. When the people charged back out of the store, they jumped into the backseat of the Infiniti and sped off. Patel—call him a Good Samaritan, a vigilante, whatever you will—stayed on the phone with 9-1-1 as he followed the car, trying to get the license plate number.

It was almost ten o'clock on that December night when the gunmen departed the store; it was dark out. Patel still gave chase. He lost sight of the car here and there; at one point, he couldn't see the Infiniti for twenty or twenty-five seconds. Later, the car was 80 then 100 feet away. When he saw the gold Infiniti again, he was *pretty* sure it was the same car. He recited the license number to 9-1-1. He didn't mention the vehicle's prominent shiny rims to the dispatcher—an omission I found useful later—but he described the driver as a "heavyset male," another detail that would become important. The Infiniti entered the freeway, and Patel drove away.

Several minutes later, a police officer spotted a gold Infiniti with a license plate number matching the one reported by Patel. He stopped the car. Deandra Jones was the slim, young woman who happened to be behind the wheel. The car contained no cash. There were no masks, no blue sweatshirts, certainly no shiny gold scarves or green backpacks. There was nothing in the car that had been seen by the victims of the robbery. The car was an Infiniti with specialized, prominent, shiny rims. Deandra sat alone in the car. She was black with a very dark complexion and wore jeans, a white sweatshirt, and bright pink tennis shoes.

The police, meanwhile, took Mrs. Wang to identify "a suspect." Parked on the side of the freeway, Mrs. Wang remained in the police car as Deandra, handcuffed and disheveled from a frenzied ride, walked into the bright lights of the police car. As soon as Deandra walked around the car, Mrs. Wang recognized the "tiptoe" way she walked. Deandra was wearing bright pink shoes, but Mrs. Wang didn't recognize those. She did recognize something familiar about "the age" of Deandra's eyes.

At her trial, Deandra Jones testified in front of a jury that she did not participate in any way in the robbery of the video store. That night, she had gone to her friend Kaya's house near the video store around 7:30. Kaya was like a sister, and Deandra had brought Tylenol for her sick son. Deandra then began to feel sick herself. After leaving Kaya's house around 10:45, Deandra drove her gold Infiniti on the freeway traveling south. She turned off the freeway to throw up; right after that, the police pulled her over.

Kaya did not testify.

The district attorney closed the case by telling the jury:

At the end of the day, you have to go home knowing you did the right thing, that the streets of [your city] are safer because of what you did in this trial. You have to go home knowing that when you're out Christmas shopping, when you step into retail establishments, when you have Christmas money in your wallet during Christmas and you're shopping, that [your city] is safer for people because you held the defendant accountable, because everything was proven beyond a reasonable doubt.

After a five-day trial, the jury took just one day to convict Deandra of all five felony counts and one misdemeanor. Deandra was sentenced to seven years and four months in state prison. Before the trial, the district attorney had repeatedly offered Deandra six months in the county jail in exchange for a guilty plea. Deandra repeatedly refused.

I called Deandra's trial attorney. "I am representing Deandra Jones in her appeal. You represented her at trial last year. Do you remember?"

She remembered Deandra well. She told me Deandra was represented earlier by another public defender. That attorney was pushing Deandra to take the plea offer. Deandra made a *Marsden* motion on her, asking the court to appoint another attorney. Deandra told the judge she was getting tons of pressure to plea. She insisted on her innocence and refused to take the offer.

"Deandra insisted on going to trial," she told me. "The other PD was going on an extended vacation."

"You didn't want to take it?"

"No, I didn't care. She turned down multiple good offers. I mean six months in jail!? But I don't care. It was her choice."

"And the trial?"

"It was going really well. Till Ms. Deandra took the stand. You'll see in the record. Actually, maybe you won't. She presented herself really well, physically, I mean. Business suit, heels, the whole thing. Looked like a middle-class girl. Then the DA played those tapes of her phone calls from jail? So ghetto. Cussing and just sounding so bad. I told her not to testify. I told her many times, but I think she was getting pressure from a guy, maybe her boyfriend. A guy her age was always coming to court, sitting and watching everything. She was so upset about this police car thing. She thought she had been kidnapped by a police officer. Thought that if she told that story to the jury, they would sympathize, I guess."

"What about the alibi?"

"She couldn't even get us her friend's address. We never got the phone number. And I mean, she was out on bail. She could have done something to help. I think we did a due diligence report on this."

"So why did you want to appeal?"

"Oh, I didn't. She did. She was pissed she got convicted." With a hint of a laugh, the attorney added, "She said she was innocent."

"You didn't believe her? The evidence might support her story."

"Oh God, that happens all the time." She chuckled, and I got a sense of eye-rolling. "I had a guy once who was caught with the gun in his hand. In his hand! Double murder. Wouldn't take a plea, just wanted a trial."

"She would turn down 180 days in jail, a nice plea, if she did it? She got over seven years."

"People just don't understand. I explained it to her so many times. She was probably involved in some way, but she was sure she wasn't *guilty* because she wasn't the one who tore into the place with a gun in her hand. She was guilty, she just didn't get it."

I didn't get it, either. I didn't understand why a smart, employed, young mother would be involved in an armed robbery. But when I really thought about it, I understood.

I remembered my own crime spree.

| | | | |

"This," I said to Jennifer as I pulled out a striped dress from the rack, "is so rad."

It was sleeveless, perfect for the scorching heat outside, and a drop waist—so in style.

"Cute with Topsiders. Or your Keds," Jennifer said.

I laid it over my arm with the other things I was going to try on. I didn't intend to buy it. I didn't have that kind of money. Jennifer had just gotten her license a few weeks before, so nothing seemed quite as thrilling as driving out to the Vintage Faire Mall by ourselves. We might end up buying an Orange Julius or a frozen yogurt; that was about all I could afford.

We wandered around, pushing hanger after hanger. I hummed along to, "Don't Stand So Close To Me," the Police song playing over the speaker system at Macy's. We all loved that song; we loved the rush of even thinking about something as rebellious as having an affair with a teacher. On a weekday afternoon, the store was empty. We headed to the dressing rooms.

I don't remember which of us decided we should take the stuff or what we said to each other; we just started shoving clothes into our purses. Mine was drawstring, brown leather, Liz Claiborne. After I was finished, it looked like a leather bowling ball on a shoulder strap. Jennifer packed hers nice and tight, and we left the dressing room.

"Act casual," I said, though my heart was beating so loud I was sure Jennifer could hear.

"Yeah, like, don't walk too fast."

I willed myself to look straight ahead. I wanted so badly to look frantically over my shoulders to see if someone was watching.

We approached the metal detectors by the doors.

We walked through.

We got past.

Nothing. No "Hey, stop," or sirens or cataclysmic earthquake—nothing kids envision might happen when they do something so immoral. Just blinding sunshine and the soft compression of heat as we pushed open the mall doors, the release of huge breaths and the rush of adrenaline as we climbed into Jennifer's Jeep and reached safety.

We sped away, windows down, screaming along with "Rox-anne," blaring from the radio.

| | | | |

If Deandra had been involved, why wouldn't she take the six-month deal? I wanted to find out from Deandra herself. We wrote each other furiously and constantly.

"Do you want to start with the night in December?"

Yes, she did.

"It was crazy. I was pulled over on the freeway. I got arrested, handcuffed, and shoved in the back of a patrol car. Then a cop jumps in, and he's going like eighty, ninety miles an hour. I was crying and yelling, but he never answered. I was so scared. Five exits later, he slams on his brakes, throwing me against the separation window and onto the ground. He seriously looks at me and goes, 'Jesus. You've been there the whole time?' I said yes and he told me he was so sorry. He said it was all a big mistake. He was gonna take me back to my car."

I didn't understand how this related to the case at all. Still, it seemed she had to get it all out.

"I already felt so bad too. I was battling with gastroparesis and spongy kidneys. I weighed about 120 pounds, the smallest I've ever been. I just had a colonoscopy the day before this happened. Believe me, I was in no condition to injure anyone."

"And you gave the information about your alibi to your attorney?"

"I did. I gave her Kaya's phone number, then later I gave her the address. Kaya was all set to come on into court and testify. She just needed a ride. She didn't know what day to come to court. Kaya has two little ones. She couldn't be in court every day. I asked my attorney if I could get someone to go pick Kaya up, and she said she couldn't."

"Do you have Kaya's contact information? I'd like to call her."

"Don't know it right off my head. But my mom, she'll know. Here's her number."

I called Deandra's mom. She gave me Kaya's number.

"I'm an attorney representing Deandra Jones," I said to Kaya. "We are appealing her convictions. Do you have a few minutes to talk?"

"Not really. I'm working now. I gotta get my kids to daycare."

"It'll just take a few minutes. Do you remember the night of December first, about two years ago? The night she was arrested?"

"Yeah."

"Was Deandra at your house?"

"Yeah."

"Do you remember why she came over?"

"Naw, she here a lot. She like family."

"Do you remember what time she came over?"

"Early in the night, but I can't remember. We was watching some reality show. *Real Chance for Love* or *Ray Jay's Reality Show*. Something like that."

"Was your son sick that night?"

"Don't remember that. But Deandra was always not feeling good. She felt sick. Kept saying how bad she was feeling."

"Have you changed your phone number recently?"

"I've been having this number for two-and-a-half years."

"What about your address. Have you moved?"

"Been here at this apartment 'bout the same time. Two-and-a-half years."

"Did the public defender or an investigator ever contact you about this case?"

"I ain't never talked to nobody."

Well, that's a pretty good alibi, I thought. She remembered details like the reality show they were watching. She lived right by the video store. We could confirm what time the show was over and know what time Deandra left. She remembered Deandra being sick.

We agreed that I would write up a declaration and mail it to her. She would sign it and mail it back. This, together with some other new evidence, would be the basis of a decent habeas petition.

A couple of searches on the internet turned up four gold Infiniti sedans with shiny rims all in the same neighborhood of the crime. I printed out the photos in color. This showed there could have been several cars in the area that fit Rahul Patel's description. If he lost sight of the gold Infiniti for as much as thirty seconds, perhaps it was not Deandra's car that he'd followed from the video store.

I also planned to submit the declaration of the trial attorney admitting that she didn't have any tactical reason for failing to object to the in-field "show up" where Deandra, handcuffed and the only suspect, was identified by Mrs. Wang. I thought an expert on eyewitness identification would have been helpful to Deandra's defense at trial. Experts are pretty much in agreement that cross-racial identifications, especially when a gun is involved and the observation is fleeting, create unreliable evidence. If the jury had heard that, it could have made a difference.

I would also argue that the district attorney committed misconduct in his closing argument when he urged the jury to convict Deandra not based on the evidence presented at the trial, but based on their fears of future crimes and his invitation to keep the streets of the jurors' hometown safer at Christmastime by convicting Deandra.

The public defender's due diligence report showed that the attorney asked her investigator to call Kaya at the same number I called. The report claimed that the investigator called that number and got a message that the number was no longer in service. He searched her name in several databases and found nothing. That was the end of the diligence.

The attorney had done a mediocre job. She did not believe that Deandra was innocent, and surely that showed at trial. She certainly hadn't given it her all—she'd rarely objected to anything. Juries *notice* this kind of thing, even if only on a subconscious level. *I* noticed, even in the transcript. It bothered me that she dismissed Deandra so easily, assuming stupidity and not innocence had motivated her to reject the plea offer. It also upset me that the attorney placed the burden on Deandra to build up her case and to gather the alibi witnesses. Something about Deandra convinced the attorney she had been involved in the crime, which had made Deandra a criminal who deserved seven years in prison.

The audio of Deandra talking to her sister from jail seemed like another person. Unlike her middle-class suited-professional exterior, the slang and profanity on the phone revealed a more abrasive side of Deandra, the "ghetto" feel that the trial attorney found problematic. For a jury, this likely meant Deandra sounded like a criminal.

Social scientists have long demonstrated that people in our society have negative associations with African Americans as a group and that those associations impact our behaviors without our conscious awareness.[4] Specifically, researchers have shown that most of us associate African Americans with crime, criminality, and violence. The inverse is true, too—we associate crime with black people.[5]

For instance, when participants in a study were primed with a black male face (seeing it for a millisecond), they were quicker to distinguish the faint outline of a weapon that slowly emerged out of a blurry series of images. So, by implicitly thinking black, they more quickly saw a weapon. When primed with drawings of weapons, participants focused on black male faces more than com-

---

4 Staats, Cheryl. "State of the Science Implicit Bias Review 2013." Kirwan Institute for the Study of Race and Ethnicity, 2013. http://kirwaninstitute.osu.edu/docs/SOTS-Implicit_Bias.pdf.

5 Eberhardt, Jennifer L. et al., "Seeing Black: Race, Crime, and Visual Processing." Journal of Personality and Social Psychology, 2004, Vol. 87, No. 6, 876 - 893.

parable white male faces. So, by implicitly thinking about weapons and violence, they more quickly identified the black person. In another study, when participants were shown the dark-skinned forearm of a masked robber, they were much more likely to interpret the ambiguous evidence presented in the mock criminal trial as indicative of guilt, *even* when they could not consciously recall the race of the defendant.

For Deandra, these associations proved disastrous. Just by hearing evidence of a violent armed robbery, the jury would tend to focus on the black face in the room—Deandra's. But by seeing Deandra, a dark-complected black woman, sitting as the defendant, sounding very "ghetto," they would have been more likely to see ambiguous evidence as indicative of a crime. Although the two main pieces of evidence against Deandra had weaknesses—the cross-racial eyewitness' identification was made with only Deandra in the line-up and the 9-1-1 caller may have reported the wrong license plate number—it would have been virtually impossible for the jury to interpret that evidence in Deandra's favor.

As the appellate attorney, I met Deandra through the unbiased lens of a written record. I didn't see her dark complexion or hear her swearing. Even handwritten letters from Deandra didn't reveal any abrasive, uncouth qualities. I related to Deandra. We were two young professional women, Central-Valley grown, who were working hard to raise two little girls.

Still, I had stolen a thousand dollars' worth of clothes without a hint of remorse. I was certainly a criminal; maybe Deandra had been involved in the robbery in some way. Maybe she was with her friends or boyfriend and didn't know what they were doing until they put on ski masks and took up guns. She had gone along when they asked for a ride to the video store. Maybe Deandra Jones was really sick of being single. It had to be hard raising two kids by herself. Maybe she was willing to do anything to keep her man. My favorite hypothesis was that her boyfriend borrowed her gold Infiniti while she sat at Kaya's watching reality TV. It explained the evidence and her insistence that she didn't commit the crime. But, only Deandra knows what really happened.

I kept working on her appeal while pursuing the habeas petition. But without a declaration from Kaya, without evidence that Deandra's original attorney had neglected to follow up on a real, solid defense that would have made a difference to the jury, I had no habeas, no real evidence outside of the record to warrant a new trial.

I called Kaya three, four, five times.

Finally, she answered: "Yeah, I got that paper you sent."

It was entirely clear that Kaya regretted answering this call.

"It would be incredibly helpful if you could sign it and send it back. I included a stamped envelope."

"I saw that."

"Do you think you could mail it back to me?"

"I just don't really wanna get involved."

"Kaya. Deandra is sitting in prison. You know her two girls, right?"

"Yeah."

"I'm sure they would really appreciate it if you would help Deandra right now."

"I wanna help, I do. It's just. I don't wanna be goin' to court."

"I understand. Look, the chances of getting back into court are so slim. Right now, we are just focused on this first small step. Going to court would be very far away, if it happened at all."

"Well . . ."

"Please, Kaya."

"Yeah, I guess I'll sign it."

"Thank you! Deandra thanks you. Do you need me to mail you another copy?"

"No, I know where it is. I got it right here."

Kaya never sent the declaration.

I talked to Deandra's mom. She was willing to do anything to help. But she had a bad back and could barely get out of bed. If I sent her a copy of the declaration, she could run it by Kaya's place, have her sign it. It turned out that Kaya was the daughter of Deandra's mother's ex-husband. They still saw each other. Kaya was still close with Deandra's half-sister, Ebony. Maybe Ebony could get it signed.

But Deandra's mom never got it signed, either.

How could I tell the court that Deandra's attorney was ineffective for failing to get Kaya to court to testify? I couldn't get the woman to sign a document and shove it into an envelope. Even if the attorney had diligently pursued this alibi, she couldn't force Kaya to cooperate.

And if I couldn't get Deandra's mother to help her, who would?

| | | | |

"Mom," I yelled from where I sat at our kitchen table, looking up from the letter in my hands. "You won't believe it. I got into Berkeley!"

It was 1990, only a couple of years since my shoplifting spree, but it looked like my friends and I were heading off to college, not prison. As a teenager, I didn't know a single person who had been arrested. I had never seen a gun except for Paw-paw's hunting rifles. But I knew something about resignation and low expectations.

I had never been to Berkeley, though we lived ninety miles away. My mom and I never talked about college. I applied because it was close and I had friends applying there. Then, I got accepted.

"Oh great, hon. How much does that cost?"

She was stirring a sauce. She didn't look up from the pot to where I sat at the table, already set with powder-blue placemats. It was probably the zucchini sauce she put on turkey loaf. When you sliced open the loaf, you saw a shiny, white, hard-boiled egg in the middle. I hated every bit of this meal.

When my mom remarried when I was seven, she really tried to be a good wife. She made dinner every night. When she divorced again, though, when I was thirteen, she brought home big buckets of fried chicken. She seemed exhausted by life and failed marriages. "This is so hard" became her mantra. Many nights after working all day as a teacher at the junior college and at the recreation department, she went straight to bed. She ate dinner under the covers watching TV so often that she kept salt and pepper shakers on her nightstand. That night, somehow, we lucked out with the turkey loaf.

"It's not that much. Tuition is like five-hundred dollars a semester. The dorms are like six thousand for the whole year."

"What about MJC? You could transfer to a better school after two years."

"People who get into Berkeley don't go to junior college, Mom."

"They do if they can't afford it. A lot of my students transfer to four-year schools. You could afford to have a car if you stayed home."

My mother taught child development courses. Her students weren't scholars; they were being trained to teach preschool. I often helped grade her papers, marveling at the run-on sentences, the lack of capitalization, and the poor spelling.

The letter in my hands wilted. I set it on the placemat that seemed cheap suddenly, its rough, woven plastic faded. It seemed impossible, but my mother had just offered to buy me a car so I could become a nursery school teacher. She might as well have invited Brad over to sit across the table and convince me not to attend any college at all. At the most, he thought UC Davis might work. Small-town Davis was like Modesto—no scary hippies, drug dealers, or criminals. No people, I had to notice, who were like my father, Hal.

Some of my mom's reluctance—and maybe a fair amount of my interest—came from the fact that Hal was living in Berkeley, getting a master's degree in mathematics. I hadn't spent much time with him, but my father was an intellectual, a graduate student at a world-renowned university. He had a serious girlfriend, a graduate student in English named Lauren. She had a halo of blonde curls and a sweet, slow way of talking. She brought stability to Hal's life. So much stability that he planned to add a Ph.D. in linguistics to his math studies. But in typical, erratic Hal fashion, he had gotten the master's in math, but now wanted to save indigenous languages.

Maybe right then and there, with my mom stirring a sauce I couldn't stand and my dropout boyfriend willing me to stay close, I decided I would join my dad and Lauren. Eventually my mom came around to the idea. She agreed to pay as much as she could afford.

When I arrived, it was clear that Hal was heavily into being Native American. He had grown his hair long and wore it in a ponytail. He painted buffalo on canvas, wrapped eagle feathers with leather, meditated on the Four Directions, and talked about Mother Earth. Maybe I wanted to be closer to him, maybe I was just looking for a way to avoid Shakespeare and *Moby Dick*, but I enrolled in Native American Studies 1A, a basic writing and liter-ature class offered instead of intro English. We read Louise Erdrich and Leslie Marmon Silko and poetry by Joy Harjo, a Muscogee/Creek woman, my family's tribe. Harjo wrote:

She had horses with full, brown thighs.
She had horses who laughed too much.
She had horses who threw rocks at glass houses. . .
She had horses who were much too shy and kept quiet in stalls of their own making. . .

Eventually, we find out, "These were the same horses."

I felt like that. I could dance courageously on tables at a bar when just that afternoon I had been fumbling around campus, a lost kid overwhelmed by a big city. I could write about respecting my grandmother, but I never phoned my mother. I tried desperately to be Native American, but felt out of place with other Native students. I could be shy in class, not talking to my classmates, then get wild drunk at football games. I talked about feminism—loud and impassioned—then hooked up with a tall, blonde guy who never returned my calls. I was not white enough, not rich like my sorority sisters, who wore diamond stud earrings to work out and talked about their summers in Europe. But I was too well-off for the Native Americans who had grown up on reservations. In some ways, I felt like I was too happy to have anything important to say. But if I had stopped to really examine what was important, I would have found that I didn't know my father at all, and I mostly felt neglected by my mother. I had been horribly taken-advantage of by boyfriends, but I had let them treat me badly.

Then, I stumbled into Doug. He was living the same conflicted, interesting life. Doug played football and was in a fraternity, but he was also a passionate environmentalist who tried to help others. Doug was too middle-class like I was, too content to gain the acceptance of Berkeley's counterculture.

He walked into my sorority during Monday Night Dinner in the early fall. He had wavy black hair, a scruffy goatee, worn-in Levi's, and handmade bracelets. He had come to talk about his program, Kick for Kids' Sake. We were to pledge a dollar or two for every field goal he made for Cal that season, all the money going to the local Big Brothers Big Sisters. I was probably impressed with his articulate pitch and his solid morals, but what I noticed most were his bright green eyes as he turned away to leave our pink house.

When I turned to a sister and asked, "Who *is* that boy?" I found out he had asked someone about me. It wasn't long before every Monday, Doug Brien was riding his bike up the hill to our house, a bunch of flowers wrapped in newspaper smashed against his handlebars. Sweaty, he'd knock on the front door and ask for me.

I loved him for being liberal but not angry, for being from a traditional family while also calling himself a "feminist." He read *Sports Illustrated* and wrote poetry, and I loved him for working hard and being generous.

During my senior year, my mom ran out of money. She sat me down at the same kitchen table, no placemats this time, and said she couldn't afford my tuition for the final semester. She said I needed to get a loan.

The financial aid office was like what I imagined of the IRS: disorganized, bureaucratic, tricky to navigate. I knew I was lucky to have escaped its forms and ominous interest rates. I tried to wade through the logistics, but after what seemed like thirty-seven forms, 103 phone calls, twelve visits to the office, and three months of waiting, I was done. I told Doug I would have to drop out of school. I would work and save the money to finish my final semester—next year.

"I'll give you the money," he said. Just like that. "I might have only barely enough, but you can have it. You shouldn't have to drop out of school."

"You can't do that. I can't take it."

He had worked all summer for that money, carrying wood and loading trucks at the local lumber shop.

"You can pay me back someday," he said. "If it comes to that."

I hugged that hippie football-playing feminist frat guy. I took the money. I needed it; I needed him.

Deandra's appeal went nowhere. The court decided that the trial attorney had done a fine job. Even if she had made some mistakes, what difference did it make? There was the eyewitness identification and there was the car. The eyewitness recognized the tiptoe way of walking that seemed unique. There could be other gold Infiniti sedans in the neighborhood, but the jury believed that the witness followed Deandra's car straight from the video store.

As a last bit of effort, I *again* asked Deandra and her mother to get me Kaya's declaration. I told them if they didn't get it, it was over. Radio silence from both women. Maybe Deandra realized that her minor involvement in the crime really was a crime. Maybe she thought she deserved her punishment. Maybe protecting the real criminals was the only safe option for her and her girls. Maybe after several years in prison, Deandra was resigned to her fate. She was halfway through her sentence. What was the point of challenging the conviction?

I was confused by these ideas, and I created stories to explain Deandra's and her family's disinterest in the appeal. Deandra could have known many people who had been in prison. Incarceration might have been the norm among her friends. She seemed to lead a double life: middle-class working mom and young black woman, but also hanging with guys from the neighborhood who carried guns. She tried to make a good life for herself and her kids, but there was no escaping the grip of the criminal justice system. Deandra, her good friend, her sister, her kids, even her mother were resigned to this life in prison.

Of course I could see how my stories about Deandra reflected my own biases about the African American community. They were the same assumptions and stereotypes which had contributed to her conviction.

I realized we weren't as alike as I thought. She was black and I was white, and that made all the difference in the criminal justice system. And although we both may have had unambitious and distracted mothers, I had Doug.

CHAPTER 5

THE RIGHT TO SILENCE

I like silence. A walk in the redwoods; the moment after the manic cat is fed, the microwave stops beeping, the panicked kid finds the hoodie or library book; when the last child closes the door on their way to school or work. Doug would say I'm overly sensitive to noise. I never fail to ask the man to lower the volume of a football game. And the ads! At night, I put a floppy, down pillow over my head to block any stray bit of night noise.

Luckily, I have never been questioned by police. They don't like silence. Not even one little bit.

"Mr. Blaylock. This is Sergeant Fuentes with the Galt police department. We are investigating a robbery of Mr. and Mrs. Anderson's home last week. Please give me a call when you get a chance."

No response. Apparently, my client, Jesse Blaylock, knew his rights. Or he was scared shitless.

You have the right to remain silent. Anything you say can and will be used against you in a court of law. You have the right to

*speak to an attorney, and to have an attorney present during any
questioning. If you cannot afford a lawyer, one will be provided
for you at government expense.*

We all know these warnings from *Law and Order* and *LA Law*
and *The Good Wife*. Since 1963, when the US Supreme Court
decided *Miranda v. Arizona*, police who arrest a suspect must
recite those words, explaining the suspect's constitutional rights.

Jesse Blaylock was silent for nearly three months. I imagined
their growing frustration.

"Jesse. Galt police, Sergeant Fuentes again."

Still, no response.

"Blaylock, this is Fuentes."

Crickets.

"Goddammit, call me back, Blaylock!"

Finally, because the police had a witness saying Blaylock had
the missing coins, they simply rang his doorbell on a Tuesday
afternoon and arrested him.

Jesse Blaylock pled not guilty and went to trial. The Andersons were like family to him. He had dated their daughter a few
years back and had stayed over at their house many times. They
had hired him to paint their house while they spent a few days at
Lake Tahoe. It really hurt Jesse that his old friends accused him of
stealing a few coins, two rings, and a rifle from the gun closet—
especially when their own daughter was the more likely suspect,
given that she had several other convictions, including one for
receiving stolen property.

A witness testified that Jesse had shown him some coins that
were the same type—Mercury-head dimes—that were taken from
the Andersons. The witness said Jesse carried them around in a
black film canister. Mr. Anderson told the jury he kept the coins in
a small silver container with a yellow lid. Even with the conflict-

ing stories, the prosecutor insisted to the jury that the containers were the same.

The prosecutor also told the jury that Jesse proved his guilt by avoiding the police. By failing to call them back, by failing to give his explanation—that he had some coins, yes, but they were not taken from the Andersons—Jesse Blaylock had shown "consciousness of guilt."

The jury believed the prosecutor. They convicted Jesse of receipt of stolen property. Even though he had not been convicted of actually stealing the coins, Blaylock got sixteen months in prison.

I got appointed by the court to represent Jesse in his appeal. I argued that the prosecutor's use of Jesse's silence—his failure to call the police back—as evidence of his guilt violated his Fifth Amendment right to remain silent.

This was not an easy argument to make. Many courts have begun to chip away at Fifth Amendment protections for defendants in police custody. Van Chester Thompkins was convicted for saying one word, "Yes," after almost three hours of silence.[6]

Police arrested Thompkins on January 10, 2000 for a shooting outside a mall in Southfield, Michigan. They gave him *Miranda* warnings. Thompkins refused to sign a form saying that he understood those rights. In two hours and forty-five minutes, Thompkins said two things: he "didn't want a peppermint," and the chair he was sitting in was "hard."

Then, after nearly three hours of a one-sided interrogation, a detective asked Thompkins whether he believed in God.

"Yes," Thompkins said.

"Do you pray to God?" asked the detective.

"Yes," Thompkins said.

---

6 *Berghuis v. Thompkins*, 560 US 370 (2010)

"Do you pray to God to forgive you for shooting that boy down?"

"Yes," Thompkins said.

Thompkins was convicted of murder.

Thompkins tried to get the final "Yes" thrown out of evidence. He argued that he invoked his "right to silence" by remaining silent for nearly three hours. The police should have stopped the interrogation long before the questions about God.

The Sixth Circuit Court of Appeals—the step below the US Supreme Court in Michigan—decided that Thompkins' "persistent silence for nearly three hours in response to questioning and repeated invitations to tell his side of the story offered a clear and unequivocal message to the officers: Thompkins did not wish to waive his rights." But the Supreme Court disagreed. The invocation of the right to silence must be invoked unambiguously and unequivocally; nearly three hours of silence is simply not enough.

Justice Sotomayor, dissenting, asked, "What in the world must an individual do to exercise his constitutional right to remain silent beyond actually, in fact, remaining silent?"[7] She concluded that Thompkins' case turned "*Miranda* upside down."

In *Salinas v. Texas*, the Supreme Court further skewered the right to silence. In 1993, Genovevo Salinas went to the Houston police station voluntarily to answer questions about a double murder of two brothers he was thought to have committed. Since Salinas was not under arrest, the police did not give him Miranda warnings. And Salinas mostly answered the officers' questions. But he said nothing when asked whether ballistics tests of the shotgun found in his home would match the shell casings found at the murder scene. He "[l]ooked down at the floor, shuffled his feet,

---

7 Cf. *Soffar* v. *Cockrell*, 300 F. 3d 588, 603 (CA5 2002) (en banc) (DeMoss, J., dissenting)

bit his bottom lip, cl[e]nched his hands in his lap, [and] began to tighten up."

Salinas was convicted of murder. Part of the evidence against him was his silence in the face of the question about the ballistics and his shuffling feet, bitten lip, clenched hands, and general tightening up. This, the prosecutor argued at trial, proved his guilt.

The Supreme Court agreed. Salinas' silence could be used against him. Salinas was not in police custody; he came to the police station "voluntarily" when they asked him to come. If Thompkins—arrested and in police custody—had to clearly and affirmatively invoke his right to silence, surely Salinas needed to be unambiguously *not silent* in his voluntary chat with police. For example: "I AM USING MY FIFTH AMENDMENT RIGHT AGAINST SELF-INCRIMINATION BY REFUSING TO ANSWER YOUR QUESTIONS, GODDAMNIT!" But, as the Supreme Court said, "popular misconceptions notwithstanding, the Fifth Amendment guarantees that no one may be compelled in any criminal case to be a witness against himself. It does *not* establish an unqualified 'right to remain silent.'"

The "'right to remain silent' that most Americans think they possess," suggests one legal scholar, simply "does not exist."[8]

Despite the losses of Van Chester Thompkins and Genevevo Salinas, I intended to challenge Jesse Blaylock's conviction and defend his Fifth Amendment rights.

| | | | |

Barely out of Berkeley, fresh from Poetry for the People, and just twenty-two, I joined the National Football League. I envisioned the NFL commissioner reading me my rights:

---

8 Maclin, Tracey. "The Right to Remain Silent v. The Fifth Amendment." University of Chicago Legal Forum, 2016, article 7.

You do not have the right to silence. You must go to loud football games with rabid fans and bad hip-hop music. You have the right to speak with the players' wives and girlfriends about designer clothes, jewelers, and whether "we" are getting enough playing time. Everything you say can and will be used to prove that you are an unsupportive girlfriend. You probably don't have the right to become an attorney. If you do decide to pursue a career in law, the NFL can and will use that against you and your boyfriend. Nothing will be provided for you at the NFL's or the government's expense.

"Things will never be the same," I finally cried to Doug, in bed after all the celebrations on the night he was drafted by the San Francisco 49ers.

We were seniors in college, and in the fall, Doug would become part of the misogynistic, violent, male-dominated culture that Berkeley poets loved to slam. It scared me to think about joining such a subculture, but it scared me more to lose Doug. I had let myself fall in love with him, but we weren't married—we were young and unsure about so much—and I worried he might move on from me, into a strange world.

"I think you're overreacting. This is a great opportunity for me—for us!"

He pulled me to our cocoon of blue flannel sheets. He kissed me, his hippie goatee scratching a little. His student apartment at Dwight Street and Piedmont Avenue felt like some kind of safe haven. It was easy to dismiss worries about the future. In the moment, I believed him.

But in the fall, it was as if I was detained in some testosterone-laden, diamond-studded alternative reality. If I wasn't rich enough for the sorority or marginalized enough for the poetry slams, I may have been the single oddest woman to ever be associated with the NFL. Just as kickers on the football team are the odd guy out, the NFL does not have a spot on the roster for part-Native-American, left-leaning, law-school-bound poets. I lived in San Francisco with friends in a funky, flat-roofed house before mid-century had made its comeback. The side table in my bedroom was a cardboard box covered with a red scarf. I worked as a research assistant for a company that consulted with government agencies about minority- and woman-owned businesses. I got up at six each morning to hustle to the bus stop to get to BART and to the office in Oakland by eight. When attending games, I wore baggy, brown linen shorts, a t-shirt, and my ancient, beloved jean jacket with tennis shoes.

I remember the wives of the very famous players who wore tight, black leather pants, black leather jackets, black high heels, and at least twenty carats worth of diamonds. NFL wives shopped for Gucci handbags; I bought a canvas messenger bag to tote books. They drove Escalades; I rode the bus. They worked out; I worked.

When I met wives after games in the players' parking lot, we had nothing to say. We stood behind ropes with red-and-gold-clad fans waving posters or glossy pictures with Sharpies in hand for autographs. Deion Sanders swaggered out in his neon blue suit with a Nehru collar. He signed a few posters and found his entourage of women in short, tight skirts and huge, gold earrings. He would lead them to the Maserati or Ferrari or Corvette, and they would tear off into the evening. Doug still drove the black Honda he had shared with his brother in high school. Because the passenger door didn't work anymore, I either crawled over the driver's seat or climbed in the window—overtones of Daisy Duke, which Doug loved.

We dated through the fall after graduation and had been together about a year when Christmas arrived. I framed a picture of us hiking in the Berkeley Hills and wrote a long card about our growing love despite major changes. As for Doug? He gave me a Reebok Step, workout clothes, and an exercise video, all courtesy of Reebok, his sponsor. The fact that it was "free" took the romance out of the jog bra and made Doug seem a little less generous than he thought he was being. I was afraid we were doomed. It became clear to me that I didn't want to fit in to this new world, but Doug wanted to explore NFL life.

While we were struggling to navigate these changes, two large envelopes arrived, each containing a letter that would change my life: the Big Envelope from Boalt, the law school at Berkeley, and the Big Envelope from Stanford. They were far too big to include one little rejection letter. With them came the thought that I would never have to worry about paying the bills again. My mom had worked so hard, never even getting health insurance because she could only get part-time jobs. Now, I understood that whatever happened with Doug or any other man I might marry, I could take care of myself. I would not be like my father, going back to school in his forties, working part time and relying on his girlfriend for support. I would not be like my mother, struggling to get by with one then two kids on her own.

Yet, when Doug and I sat down to talk over my choices, the echoes of my mother's Berkeley reaction were impossible to ignore.

"But baby," he said, even as he reached across to take my hand, "Boalt is just as good."

Doug might have been intrigued by NFL life, but he was a middle-class guy, and a frugal one at that. Private schools and crazy tuitions just didn't fit into his worldview.

"Well, no. Not really. Stanford is ranked third nationwide; Boalt is tenth or eleventh."

"But in the Bay Area, everyone knows they're both amazing schools."

"Stanford has a much smaller class. That would be so nice."

"You're a Berkeley girl. You don't want to deal with private school stuff."

Did he picture me feeling bad about jumping into his crusty Prelude with the broken passenger door and pulling into a parking space next to a snotty trust-fund kid in a convertible Mercedes?

"I would love a break from all the bureaucracy of a big school. Not having to wait in huge lines and fight for everything."

"Stanford costs three times as much."

"Does everything always come down to money for you?"

"How come it never does for you?"

"I care about cost. It's just not everything."

The decision infested my everything. I talked to everyone I knew and everyone they knew. I talked to criminal lawyers and corporate lawyers and friends who had sisters-in-law whose neighbors knew someone who went to Boalt or Stanford. A successful lawyer I worked with—soft-spoken, yet powerful, impeccably put-together, yet friendly—said, "You attend the best school you are admitted into, period. There is no choice to be made." She'd gone to Harvard. This seemed like territory she knew. Good lawyers know a good lawyer when they meet one, and I knew for certain she was a good lawyer.

Doug was not a lawyer, but his voice rang louder than all the others.

| | | | |

The day, years later, when Doug called to say he needed a lawyer to respond to the federal government's subpoena, he needed me in an entirely new way. I had gone to countless NFL games. I had learned the rules of football! I cheered for him and hugged him after he missed big kicks. But I never belonged in the NFL, and I'd never seemed to help him in the right way. Where does one get training on what to say to your dearest love after he misses the game-winning field goal that means his team will not, in fact, go to the Super Bowl? Somehow, I had never gotten that training.

I never felt quite good enough at supporting him through those moments. I didn't know what to say and Doug—with his stoicism and his even-keeled nature—never seemed to need me to say it. It didn't feel like he had ever really needed me. Until that day.

We knew he needed an attorney, but we also knew I couldn't be that attorney. I called the best criminal defense attorney I knew, maybe one of the best in the country. We had met at receptions of women lawyers but didn't really know each other. I was actually afraid she might remember me for missing a deadline that her partner, Ted, had helped me fix. But it turned out she remembered me as Christy's friend. Christy and I had gone to law school together, and Christy now worked for Cris.

Cris was already familiar with the investigation into the bidders on the courthouse steps. She told me that companies all over the Bay Area and Sacramento were scrambling for attorneys. She was sorry, but she was unable to represent Doug because of a conflict. She did say that we needed to find another attorney: "And you should find one today."

Her urgency put a pit in my stomach. She recommended a federal-court specialist named Michael.

"If this were you, this is the person you'd hire?" I asked.

"Absolutely."

Something about the conviction in her voice, in her urgency, and in the way I wanted to trust her made me start to cry. I tried to hide the sound, but I know she recognized the long silence. I attempted a brief thank you and hung up the telephone.

Jesse Blaylock's silence—his failure to call the police back countless times—and the prosecutor's use of his silence to prove his guilt unambiguously violated his Fifth Amendment rights.

This was the determination of the California Court of Appeal. I was shocked.

The Court of Appeal reasoned that the prosecutor's argument and evidence of Jesse's failure to return the officer's calls "deprived [the] defendant of any meaningful right to refuse to talk to the police." Even as the court acknowledged that prior court decisions had not agreed, saying that silence *before* someone is arrested *may* be used as evidence of their guilt, the present court was making a major extension to the legal protections for defendants' right to silence in California.

It amazed me further when the court found that the legal error of the prosecutor using Jesse's silence as evidence of guilt had actually affected the jury's decision to convict him. This was not a "harmless error," as so many legal errors were. "It is difficult to deem an error 'unimportant' where, as here, the evidence in support of defendant's conviction was minimal," the court explained.

The court then reversed Jesse's conviction.

The DA could charge him again, but that surely wouldn't be worth taxpayer dollars. Jesse had already served his sixteen-month sentence in state prison, but he was elated with the reversal. The felony would be off his record.

He emailed to thank me for my work. He seemed to understand the full weight of having the felony removed. He was hoping to find a job as a painter. I was happy for him, of course, but there was no way Jesse Blaylock could have known the impact he had on me as a lawyer. I basked, secretly, in our victory. I kept it close, at the forefront of my consciousness, so I could remind myself that I had worked hard and had achieved a significant victory—all while unbuckling a toddler from her car seat for the sixteenth time in one day. It became an almost physical feeling, like a small smooth pebble in my pocket to touch when I read that former classmates were getting important appointments in D.C. and students at Stanford were having cert petitions granted by the Supreme Court. I was a good lawyer. I was someone who helped people.

In fact, I helped protect people from the force and weight of the United States government. I defended the Constitution. Even if the right to silence is as fictional as *LA Law*, the Fifth Amendment protects us from self-incrimination.

After the evening when Doug and I first discussed his case in the hot tub, we simply did not talk about "the legal situation." Maybe logistics or surface issues—finding a lawyer was the priority—but we didn't touch on what happened, not Lance or the other bidders, not what constituted fraud, not what Doug knew or didn't know. In retrospect, it was strange that we couldn't speak when we were usually good about sharing this kind of thing. I think we were just too scared. The reality felt too grave.

CHAPTER 6

THE RIGHT TO
(BE) COUNSEL

Dear Ms. Brien:

I see from your State Bar profile that you went to Stanford Law School. You have been appointed to represent me. Can you tell me how many cases you've won reversal in?

Thank you,
Dorothy Crenshaw

Well, this was awkward. How do I tell my new client that I've won exactly one case?

Dorothy Crenshaw and I eventually met at the Santa Clara County Superior Court. I waited in a crowded line to go through the metal detector. Attorneys who came here every day hustled through their line. The rest of us waited, sweating, unloading belts and coins and shoes and phones onto the convey-

or. A layer of grime coated the linoleum and the walls, and there was the smell of mildew covered with bleach. None of us really wanted to be there. Going to trial court invariably involved a lot of waiting around and asking for extensions. Rarely did anything consequential get done. I wore my brown pantsuit. (My black skirt suit was reserved for more serious occasions.)

I walked down the crowded hallway looking for courtroom 12. All that law school, all those all-nighters, all that tuition, to wander a malodorous government building in search of a client who didn't seem to trust me, who was assigned to me by the court, who had already peppered me with daily calls about code sections and misspellings in the court record—all before we'd even met.

"Would you happen to be the attorney Shanti Brien?" A middle-aged woman in a puffy floral dress approached me.

So, this was Dorothy: long, gray hair parted down the middle, hunched shoulders, and head bowed over a legal file clutched in her hands. The thing was six inches thick, exploding with papers, Post-Its, and receipts. You might have taken her for an ex-hippie or soft-spoken librarian. She may have been a former protestor, but she was also a lawyer and mother who supported her adopted nine-year-old daughter by working as a contract attorney. She was also a convicted felon.

| | | | |

The eerie thing was that Dorothy Crenshaw couldn't have looked more like Barbara Babcock, who, on my first day at Stanford Law School, stood tall before my class in the packed auditorium and cried out, "You've arrived!"

Professor Babcock reassured us that we did not need to stress or fight to the death with classmates for the best grades. We had earned admittance into one of the best law schools in the country, and we should soak in that knowledge. We should maybe even have a good time doing it.

"You," she reiterated, "have made it!"

The "first" woman in many of her posts, Professor Babcock was a bit of a legal celebrity. She was the leader of the Civil Rights Division of the Justice Department and then professor at Stanford. I was dizzy and wanted to throw up; I wanted so badly to do well. In Babcock's civil procedure class, I sat inconspicuously up in the left corner. My friend Michael sat next to me on my left, bespectacled and always giddy with the thrill and challenge of another day of law school.

Professor Babcock had been a public defender before coming to Stanford. She loved trials. She spoke of them with nostalgia and a sweet, slightly-southern twang. She didn't have the sarcasm or toughness that people associate with trial attorneys. Criminal defense lawyers especially have the reputation of being brash and loud or slick-talking and smooth. Babcock was neither; she just appreciated the art of telling one person's story, telling her client's story so the jury understood and had compassion for another person in a tough spot.

Professor Babcock was kind; she empathized with our stress and massive anxiety. She spoke slowly. Her voice matched the soft curls that framed her wide, welcoming face. But her Justice Department credentials and tenured professorship at Stanford Law School meant she was brilliant, too, no question. I wanted to be her.

I got an externship as a public defender in Oakland.

"In summary, Your Honor, my argument is that the defendant did not cause the great bodily injury, but instead, the victim is responsible for her own injuries. She is the one who decided to jump out the window. There were other, far less dramatic and dangerous ways for her to leave the fight she was in with the defendant."

This concluded my argument as a certified student extern in the Alameda County Superior Court. A second-year law student, but with the right to defend people in the trial court (as long as a public defender closely supervised me).

I may have been happy enough with classes at Stanford, but this client and his girlfriend pulled my attention in a way Advanced Legal Writing just couldn't. I prepared my argument for weeks; it was not a legally complex one, but it was my first, and in front of a real judge.

The courtroom was crowded with defendants shackled in orange jumpsuits, uniformed bailiffs with big beer bellies yawning with boredom, and court reporters in tight skirts typing frantically. I had on my only suit, a light blue silk more appropriate for a wedding than the courtroom. I'd pulled my long hair back in a bun, trying to transform from pseudo-hippie student to lawyer.

Family members, girlfriends, and babies filled the wooden benches to capacity. Almost exclusively, lawyers came to the podium when they heard their case name—"People versus Jones!"— yelled out by the courtroom clerk, where they asked for more time. "A continuance" was the most favorite request.

When my case was called, I sped to the table, nervous. The whole crowded court paused. I wasn't asking for any cookie cutter continuance or arraignment. I was actually going to say something.

I began slowly. The judge interrupted and asked questions, genuinely interested.

"I will take this matter under submission," he ended formally, then added, "You did a fine job, young lady."

I smiled. "Thank you, Your Honor."

I turned toward the restless crowd of defendants and girlfriends and lawyers and parents. Halfway down the aisle, a big African American guy flapped his hand out toward me.

"Excuse me, ma'am." He wore a tie he may have borrowed from a dead uncle. "Can I have one of your cards?"

"Oh my gosh! Thank you!" I said, completely unprofessional. "I'm just a law student. I don't have any cards, and I can't really represent you."

When he looked disappointed, turning his attention back to the judge who kept the chaos rolling, I understood that I could be a good lawyer. Young and inexperienced, I could still craft an argument and help people stuck in this sweaty mass of humanity, caught in the churning criminal justice system.

| | | | |

I sat with Dorothy Crenshaw in courtroom 12, the large doors of the judge's chambers muffling the chaos. It didn't comfort me that Dorothy had tried to fire her trial lawyer before her convictions, but our first order of business together was to recreate what was said at that hearing. The transcripts of the attempted firing were missing, and I needed a complete record of what happened at trial.

Dorothy and I sat straight in the hard, wooden chairs. I looked nervous, like a young kid dressed up as an attorney. She looked out-of-place, too, like a Dead Head at the symphony opening.

For eighteen years, Dorothy had lived in a condominium complex full of young Silicon Valley types. Only she'd had the time to worry about the homeowners' association and its annual meetings, officer elections, two bank accounts, and the Statements of Information filed annually with the California Secretary of State. Dorothy was like the mom who makes you wear matching outfits, the low-level manager who demands useless reports, the DMV. And she lived next door.

"Dorothy manipulated me," one of the owners testified at the trial. "She made my life upside down with ridiculous requests. No, I did not like her."

One day, the other owners had held a meeting without telling Dorothy, and they'd voted her out of office. Later, Dorothy transferred money from the association account to the reserve account to satisfy a title company request for proof that the association had enough in reserves. She had been acting as secretary and treasurer—no one else was doing it. Everyone had bent the homeowners' association rules, but who cared?

When another owner found out, he'd called the police to say the money had been stolen. Turns out the police cared. The district attorney cared.

But a jury didn't care. By acquitting Dorothy of the theft charge, they sent a message to the district attorney that the theft prosecution was a waste of time and resources.

But two other charges stuck. On two occasions, Dorothy filed Statements of Information with the Secretary of State, and she signed them as secretary and chief financial officer of the homeowners' association. Given that Dorothy was no longer an officer of the homeowners' association at the time of the filing (because she had been secretly voted out of office), she had lied on the forms filed with the State. The jury convicted Dorothy of two counts of "filing false instruments."

Two felonies. Dorothy would lose her law license after all.

In courtroom 12, I tried to get the appeal of those felonies moving.

The judge jumped right in; he wanted to get through this quickly. "First, Ms. Crenshaw will explain to us why she wanted to relieve Mr. Richards, and then Mr. Richards will respond, trying to provide the same reasons that he provided in the hearing that day."

"I hired Mr. Richards," Dorothy said. "I paid him $25,000, which is more than I make in a year. He assured me that he had a personal relationship with the district attorney and that he could get the case to 'go away.' Right before trial, he had done virtually nothing."

She barely took a breath.

"He wanted me to take a deal of two misdemeanors. But I couldn't take that; I would lose my law license because theft is a crime of moral turpitude, even if it is a misdemeanor. Plus, I had been offered that deal even before I hired him."

I felt that I should interject, do something lawyerly for her, but my client was really getting riled up.

"He did not plan on calling important witnesses. He was not prepared for trial. He wouldn't even listen to me about my idea for my defense. Our working relationship had deteriorated beyond repair. I needed a different attorney. My livelihood and my daughter were on the line."

"Thank you, Mrs. Crenshaw," the judge muttered, annoyed. Dorothy had that effect on people.

Then it was Mr. Richards' turn to respond. At least sixty-five years old with a solid dome of gray hair, he was an imposing attorney in a dark gray suit. He let it all out.

"Your Honor. I was ready for trial. I listened to her ideas for a corporate or business defense. I just chose not to use them. Strategy decisions are mine to make!"

He jabbed his finger at her then at himself. He had hundreds of other cases he could be working on but was stuck here with Dorothy when he thought this trial was behind him.

"I told Dorothy she should take the deal! She should have, obviously. It was a great deal, a misdemeanor or two. I can't help it if she wouldn't. I was ready for trial, it just didn't go her way," he ended with what seemed like a tinge of satisfaction, knowing she was stuck with two felonies because she hadn't taken his advice.

We sat in uncomfortable silence until the judge finally spoke.

"Given that Ms. Crenshaw hired Mr. Richards, she would normally have the right to change attorneys at her discretion. However, we were on the eve of trial. I did not think the relationship had deteriorated to the point where Mr. Richards would not be effective. He is an excellent attorney. I knew he would be prepared. I thought the disruption of the judicial process outweighed Ms. Crenshaw's choice of counsel at this late stage."

And with that, our preliminary proceeding was over. We would have a record of the dispute between Dorothy and her lawyer, and

I would use it later, writing the appeal. It wouldn't be a major issue, ultimately, but I felt I had let Dorothy down. I should have said something to defend her. Between the judge and Mr. Richards— two imposing, gray-haired men, decades of legal work between them—I just couldn't.

Walking out of the courthouse, Dorothy wanted to talk more, discuss what went wrong, what I should focus the appeal on.

"I know you must be so busy, but . . . do you have time to get a cup of coffee . . . or something?" she asked.

I never did that with clients. (They were usually in prison.) But I wasn't really that busy, and I knew an hour's investment might save me a lot of grief from Dorothy later.

We walked to the local IHOP and sat in a vinyl booth made for two people. The coffee tasted like dirty water.

After more than an hour of discoursing on legal strategy, Dorothy's head suddenly hung toward her cold coffee.

"This whole thing has taken such a toll."

She pulled strands of lank, gray hair away from her forehead and tucked them behind her ear.

"I guess I can't really imagine what it's like," I said, years before I was forced to imagine my husband as a felon. I couldn't think of losing my law license either; I had just gotten my career started.

"The money, for one thing. I paid that darn attorney twenty-five thousand dollars. I'm completely bankrupt. Besides, I can't get a job. Once you have a felony, you have to put that down on every application."

I knew this was a crippling consequence of a felony.

"I might have to take my daughter out of dance lessons."

Dorothy dug in her purse and pulled out a picture of a chubby young girl in a leotard and tutu. She looked mixed-race; her hair was light brown, curly and soft around her face.

"I adopted her four years ago. She loves dance more than anything in the world."

I could see true despair in Dorothy's face as she tucked the picture back in her purse. I felt the weight of my responsibility to this woman and her daughter; they counted on me to win the appeal.

One of my arguments was that the district attorney's evidence should not have been admitted. The DA used only the minutes from the homeowners' association meeting the other owners had held without telling Dorothy to show that Dorothy was not secretary and chief financial officer of the association when she said she was. But the minutes were hearsay.

Hearsay is a complicated rule that law students spend at least half a semester learning. The official definition is "an out-of-court statement used to prove the truth of what is stated." For example, I could not go to court as a witness and testify that "Zach told me that he saw Lilli sneaking candy" to help prove the case against Lilli. Zach's out-of-court statement is hearsay; he would have to come to court himself and testify to what he saw so that he could be cross-examined about it and the jury could evaluate his trustworthiness as a witness. However, I *could* testify that "Zach told me that he saw Lilli sneaking candy" to prove that Zach liked to tell on his sisters. It is also an out-of-court statement, but it is not used to prove that Lilli sneaked candy, it is used to prove what Zach did.

But this is not what happened with the homeowners' association minutes. The DA submitted them, a recording of out-of-court statements, to prove exactly what the minutes said—that Dorothy was voted out of office and that she was not the secretary and the chief financial officer. The DA said the minutes constituted an exception to the rule stating that minutes of corporate meetings are exempt from the hearsay rule. Still, corporation minutes, like other business records, must be shown to be inherently trustworthy before a jury may consider them.

I told the Court of Appeal that the minutes were not trustworthy at all. They were written and certified by the same people accusing Dorothy of stealing association money. And only after the DA asked the accusers to certify them to prepare Dorothy's prosecution.

The Court of Appeal agreed—about one of the sets of minutes. Because one homeowner, even though he was an accuser, actually attended the second meeting and signed the minutes as accurate, the court concluded that those were trustworthy.

One of Dorothy's felony convictions was reversed. Victory! One was upheld. Tragedy. She would still lose her law license and she would still have to write "felony" on every job application. Dorothy was blunt about her disappointment.

Re: Sucky decision in my case

Dear Shanti:

I found the decision. It's about what we expected after listening to oral argument . . .

As I mentioned, my preference would be for a motion for reconsideration, as well as a petition for review—while I understand that is not the usual course, such a two-pronged approach would give me a better shot at a full reversal.

Here are my four reasons for seeking reconsideration:

[Lengthy and omitted].

FYI, there may be a bit of poetic justice here, as apparently both [of the young homeowners] are in foreclosure and hopefully soon out of the Association.

Thanks for all your help,

Dorothy

Poetic or not, I did not feel that justice had been done. This was a homeowners' association dispute that turned south. As annoying as Dorothy was, did she deserve to lose her livelihood as an attorney and to be forced into bankruptcy because she said she was the secretary? Did her adopted daughter deserve to lose the one healthy, fun activity in her life because the neighbors were mad at her mom? I did not think so.

But these types of crimes and convictions have exploded in our country. In *Three Felonies a Day: How the Feds Target the Innocent*, Boston lawyer Harvey Silvergate estimates that most Americans unknowingly commit three felonies a day. Doubling the speed limit, cheating on your spouse, acting drunk in public, buying something from eBay or Craigslist that was stolen—all crimes. More and more seemingly innocent activities—like signing as the secretary of a homeowners' association when you perform all of the secretarial duties—have become crimes. And because legislatures and prosecutors have put less emphasis on requiring an intent to commit a crime, they have won more and more convictions.

Congress creates about fifty new criminal laws each year. This means there are over 4,500 federal criminal laws in 27,000 pages of the United States federal code. We have criminalized addiction, criminalized poverty, criminalized homelessness, and criminalized mental illness. We have criminalized youth and normal teenage behavior so much that someone invented the term "school to prison pipeline." The rush of kids through the pipeline has slowed in recent years, but we still lock away more than 50,000 kids on any given day,[9] thousands for "status" offenses like running away, truancy, and "incorrigibility."

---

9 Sawyer, Wendy. "Youth Incarceration: The Whole Pie 2019." The Prison Policy Initiative, February, 2018. https://www.prisonpolicy.org/reports/youth2018.html.

Overall, our criminalization addiction has led us to rock bottom. Even after some moderate reforms, in 2019, the American criminal justice system holds almost 2.3 million people in state and federal prisons, local jails, and other facilities. It seems like we are all criminals, will be criminals someday, or could become criminals—if we're not ridiculously scrupulous. All it takes is a simple signature, the click of a mouse, another glass of chardonnay, or a nod at a guy named Lance who assumes you are in on a bid-rigging conspiracy.

Progress has been made—partly, I imagine, because no one has escaped the insatiable appetite of the criminal justice system. We've either been arrested or convicted, know someone who has, or read an article/seen a movie about a person sent to prison for something we've done, almost done, or wanted to do. This includes politicians. Elected officials from both parties have come together to pass some federal reforms, including the First Step Act in late 2018. But the real work will be in the states.

Eventually, to really address the problem, we must reconsider punishments and sentences for all crimes, including the "violent" ones. Michelle Alexander, in her seminal book *The New Jim Crow*, recognizes this as part of the solution to our hyper-incarceration rates. Yet, this is politically and practically challenging. It's often hard to tell a nonviolent offender from a violent offender. Is a marijuana dealer who brandishes a switchblade a violent criminal? How about the getaway driver in an armed robbery? And what if someone now serving time for a minor drug offense has a prior conviction for aggravated assault? These are tough questions that we could address—and someday must address—but we don't seem quite ready.

For now, it seems best to start with the easiest, simplest of reforms: the mass de-criminalization of common, minor actions. Possessing and using marijuana is a good start. Drug crimes still result in the incarceration of almost half a million people. Even today, police make over one million drug possession arrests each year. "Drug arrests continue to give residents of over-policed communities criminal records, hurting their employment prospects and increasing the likelihood of longer sentences for any future offenses."[10]

Poverty is a close second. About 500,000 people are in jail with no conviction or sentence because judges denied them bail or they cannot afford the bail that was set. It is unclear how many, but the excessive imposition of fees and fines (and harsh practices to enforce those debts) ensnarl thousands of additional people long after they have completed their sentences. Crimes of living on the street, loitering, and others related to housing insecurity and homelessness also punish people for being poor.

Finally, we must decriminalize addiction and mental illness. These afflictions often lead to criminal behavior like petty theft, public intoxication, and simple assault—endless arrests, plea deals, short jail stays, and probation will never lead to a cure. Even with half a million people incarcerated for drug offenses, drug-related deaths hit a record high of 72,000 in 2017. That is 200 deaths every day! Almost two decades ago, Portugal decided to treat drug addiction as a health crisis rather than a crime. The country has made remarkable strides, with the rate of drug-related deaths the lowest of most western countries (six per million compared with 60 per million in Britain and 312 per million in the US). They happen to save their country billions of dollars each year, too. [11]

---

10 Sawyer, Wendy and Peter Wagner. "Mass Incarceration: The Whole Pie 2019." The Prison Policy Initiative, March, 2019. https://www.prisonpolicy.org/reports/pie2019.html.

11 "The [Portuguese] Health Ministry spends less than $10 per citizen per year on its successful drug policy. Meanwhile, the US has spent some $10,000 per household (more than $1 trillion) over the decades on a failed drug policy that results in more than 1,000 deaths each week." Nicolas Kristoff. "How to Win a War on Drugs: Portugal treats addiction as a disease not a crime." The New York Times, Sept. 22, 2017.

I can't begin to guess how much Dorothy Chrenshaw's case cost the taxpayers of California. The resources spent on the investigation, prosecution, and criminal supervision of this middle-aged mom kind of blew my mind. And for being in a homeowners' association dispute! It seemed unfair and ridiculous and wasteful and unjust, all at once. Dorothy could be every middle-aged woman in America. She could be your dental hygienist or your son's first grade teacher or the lawyer writing up your mortgage. She could be any of us, and now, instead of an attorney, she was a felon. It hit me that *anyone* could become a felon.

CHAPTER 7

ASSISTANCE OF COUNSEL

"This is a picture of my son," Scott Mendoza said as he slid a photo across the table.

Mr. Mendoza wore jeans, a freshly-pressed shirt, and cowboy boots. He owned an auto service station about three hundred miles north of San Francisco. He was a regular guy—except that his son was in prison for life for murder. And he was responsible, even if only in the slightest way.

The picture showed Scott, his son Jake, and his four other sons; someone had snapped the picture during a family visit at the prison. Jake wore the standard-issue chambray shirt in the standard style—buttoned to the top—and bagging dark jeans. Scott looked calm in the picture, but he seemed nervous meeting me here in the law library of a formal legal office, with dark mahogany furniture and hundreds of legal books looming over us. I had borrowed the fancy office in Marin from an attorney friend; I worked from home, and it seemed unprofessional to meet a potential client at a Starbucks.

"He's so handsome," I told Scott.

It was true—Jake was striking. The oldest and tallest of the boys, Jake had cropped light brown hair, a strong jaw, and wide-set eyes. He smiled wide. He looked so happy to see his father and his brothers. Scott was smiling, too. He and Jake gripped each other tightly around the waist.

The two younger boys, about seven and eight, stared big-eyed at the camera. But the older boys, sixteen and seventeen, looked tough. Maybe even a bit resigned, like they suspected someday they would join their older brother.

"The picture is for you," Scott insisted as I tried to push it back across the dark table. He almost whispered, "Please help us."

Two years earlier, Jake's attorney, Clara Thompson, had asked the judge to clear the courtroom during the middle of Jake's trial. She needed to talk privately with Jake and his father.

"We're talking about a possible resolution?" the judge clarified.

"Yes," she said.

"Why don't we do this," suggested the judge. "We'll clear the courtroom with the exception of Ms. Thompson. The defendant can stay. If his father can submit to a pat search, he can sit at that table. They can talk. The rest of us will leave the room for a few minutes. If that's acceptable."

This was not a question but an order.

The jurors shuffled out, probably happy to stand, stretch, check their phones and get out of the stuffy space. Once judge, court recorder, and clerk had moved through the door, Ms. Thompson looked at Jake and told him he should take the DA's last offer—second degree murder. Fifteen-years-to-life.

"But," she added, "you'll only have to serve seven."

Jake was interested. He had pushed for twelve years, without "to-life." He knew he had committed a crime, stabbing a man in a parking lot of a bar. He understood that it was a mistake even to carry a knife. But the guy had lunged at *him*. He couldn't swallow sitting in prison the rest of his life for that, putting the possibility of his freedom in the hands of the parole board. He had been in jail long enough to know that it should be called the denial-of-parole board. More than one inmate had told him that taking a life sentence meant he was "fucked." He liked this new plan. He would do his seven years and be done.

Scott remembers being exhausted. He recalls how much his head and back and shoulders ached and that his son felt the need to talk to him alone. Jake told their attorney he needed to "sleep on it."

Ms. Thompson promised to confirm his eligibility for parole after seven years.

Scott remembered her being "pretty sure" he would be eligible. She felt the best part was that the DA would also agree not to oppose his parole. She explained that what the DA wanted had a big impact on the board's decision. She planned to meet with Scott and Jake the next day.

Once the judge and jury returned, Ms. Thompson relayed what had happened during the private meeting for the record: "I need to determine whether or not penal code section 3046 indicates that with a fifteen-to-life, whether that fifteen would be deemed under the statute to be the minimum period that he would have to serve. I believe that's not the case."

Neither Scott nor his son followed what seemed like a bunch of legalese.

"I think the subdivisions of that statute talk about—there are numerous other portions of the penal code, they will have a certain maximum period of time potential or a life-tail, but will say out of that they have to serve a specific period of time. I don't see that here." Ms. Thompson went on and on. "I'm going to try to confirm with the State if Mr. Mendoza would in fact be eligible for consideration for parole after seven years. I think he is, but I just want to make sure. Even though technically that might be a collateral consequence. I think that is important."

Jake really didn't understand those words, "collateral consequence," he just knew that he could get out in seven years.

Back in court the next day, in a bit of a hurry, Ms. Thompson mentioned to Jake that he wouldn't get good-time or work-time credits.

Jake trusted the experience and efficiency of his attorney. This detail seemed like "no big deal."

"The sentence will be fifteen-years-to-life," she explained.

Jake remembered thinking that this was what she had said before. It sounded like the better deal. He looked down at the table, then took a quick glance behind him to where his dad sat.

Then he said to Clara Thompson, "I'll take it."

She smoothed her suit jacket and addressed the judge: "Mr. Mendoza is prepared at this time to enter a plea of guilty to murder in the second degree with the understanding that as a result of that—this is clearly a strike offense and because it is a murder charge, under 2933.2, he is not entitled to any good-time or work-time credits."

She continued to explain the other details of the deal. The DA agreed that was the deal. The judge confirmed that Jake understood. He thought he did.

What Jake did not understand was that no good-time credits meant that he had no chance of getting out in seven, ten, or even twelve years. He would live in prison for at least fifteen years. After fifteen years, he would see the parole board, but chances were very slim that he would win freedom.

Jake's attorney simply hadn't explained. One day, she talked about parole in seven years; the next day, she talked about good-time and work-time credits. This twenty-year-old high-school graduate did not realize the crucial legal connection. Everyone in the courtroom with any kind of legal training understood that he would serve at least fifteen years. Jake and his father had no idea.

| | | | |

As a young lawyer—inexperienced and naive, idealistic and green—I had no idea what was going on, either.

The partner at the prestigious New Orleans law firm was a small man with dark hair (clearly cut weekly) and small, round glasses. He was obviously smart and extraordinarily conservative. His red tie probably cost as much as the one suit I owned as a first-year associate. I think he was from Louisiana, but he acted like he was East Coast, voice clipped, when he said, "You requested to speak with me?"

After graduating law school—Doug and I married during my second year—I followed him to New Orleans, where he played for the Saints. I'd been a committed "public interest" law student, especially dedicated to criminal law. New Orleans, however, didn't have a public defender system. If people accused of crimes couldn't afford attorneys, the court would assign a private criminal defense attorney to the case. The attorney made only a couple hundred dollars representing the person, even if the case went to trial and involved hundreds of hours of work.

This system contributed to the meteoric increase in Louisiana's prison population. In 1978, Louisiana incarcerated 179 people per 100,000, about the same as most other states. (In comparison, England and Wales incarcerated 41.8 people per 100,000 at that time.) By 1999, when I moved to Louisiana, the rate had reached almost 800 people per 100,000. Even Russia and China couldn't match Louisiana's zeal for imprisonment. Russia's rate was 492—about the same as California's and the United States' rates—and

China's 119.[12] Louisiana continues to reign as the international king of incarceration.

But I didn't have the courage or confidence—as a brand-new attorney, an awkward NFL wife, a Louisiana newbie—to take on prison reform and the complicated legal and social forces supporting the state's dysfunction. And I had student loans to pay off.

I sent my resume to a couple of big firms.

One fell in love with the "Stanford" on my resume. They took the top graduates from Tulane and Loyola, but Stanford was a different league—a rare, exotic nugget of prestige for the engraved look-who-we've-hired announcements that go out in the South each fall.

The firm occupied a large, brick building on an oak-lined street of New Orleans. Massive, white doors intimidated visitors, and the lobby dripped marble and gold leaf. Just past the monumental curving staircase, a creaking ironwork elevator delivered dark-suited lawyers to mahoganied offices.

I got my own secretary and half a paralegal. We ate at the best restaurants in the city, often on the firm's tab. Turtle soup and crab cakes, bread pudding with buttery brandy sauce—for lunch! I felt like I lived in a John Grisham novel. Plus, they promised me all of the criminal cases that came in the door.

"Yes, sir," I muttered to the bespectacled partner. "I . . . I . . . just wanted to say . . . I don't think . . . about the tobacco case. I don't think I can do it."

I wore a dark suit and black pumps, but not the required nylons. Word had it the firm would drop mandatory stockings for the sticky hot summers, but at this point, I was the rebel associate with bare legs from wacky California.

---

12 "Trends in US Corrections." The Sentencing Project, 2017. https://www.sentencing-project.org/publications/trends-in-u-s-corrections/.

He looked at me with pity and nostalgia, like he remembered being young and caring. On the expanse of dark wood between us sat a neat stack of papers, a gold pen, and a picture of two kids in an awkward pose. Big Tobacco litigation was the firm's most lucrative work. It would require decades of billable hours, and he needed most of the new associates on the case.

"That's fine," he said.

Two days later, I was assigned to work on PCB.

Polychlorinated biphenyls (PCBs) were used liberally as a coolant and a lubricant in electrical transformers and capacitors before the 1970s. In humans, exposure to PCBs can cause a skin reaction known as chloracne, bleeding and neurological disorders, liver damage, spontaneous abortions, malformed babies, cancer, and even death. Because PCBs were used on a massive scale before being outlawed, junkyards filled with refrigerators, air conditioners, and other everyday products became unregulated toxic waste sites, leaking toxins into the groundwater of neighborhoods and creating deadly playgrounds for children.

I was charged with defending the manufacturers of this toxic product. When I took the job with the firm, they had promised me all the criminal cases; I never figured the criminals would be malformed-baby-causing toxin producers.

I didn't lead the defense, create strategy, or even talk to the clients. I cut and pasted denials and objections from previous documents created by the firm. The fact-gathering (or "discovery") phase of the litigation would take years. Corporate litigation is a big game of evasion and delay. The Big Firm was the king, and I was his pawn.

I fantasized about defending a kid that had robbed a store to pay his rent. I did some pro bono work for a young Cajun man with a childhood full of abuse. I even travelled to Angola Prison with a partner at the firm to meet the young man and sit in on a hearing. But pro bono work didn't pay my big firm salary—PCB makers did.

During law school, I had spent a summer at the Prison Law Office. It was the kind of work that allowed me to help an imprisoned man marry the woman he loved, even when the prison mistakenly believed he was already married. The Office currently resides on the cutting edge of prison litigation and reform, but when I was there, it was a hole-in-the-wall across the highway from San Quentin.

I remembered San Quentin so well—the castle-like building at the edge of the San Francisco Bay, the decaying structure surrounded by glistening blue water. Our group of eager interns toured the place, having been told to wear pants and button-down shirts, nothing too revealing and nothing blue. The inmates wore blue. I saw chipped paint and rusty metal. Men shuffled in the dirt yard, following us with their eyes as we moved above in a fenced walkway. I didn't feel afraid; I was fascinated. The freshness, freedom, and openness I had felt when driving over the Richmond–San Rafael Bridge was eclipsed by monotony, helplessness, and frustration the moment I entered those gates.

There was something real and raw, something mesmerizing about prison. The inmates I met and helped were so thankful, so courteous and kind, that I couldn't help but be attracted to this other world.

Only two years after helping disabled prisoners get access to meals and medical attention with the Prison Law Office, I was stuck at the Big Firm, cutting and pasting objections from Requests for Admissions and whatever else the partners asked. I billed by ten-minute increments, defended the PCB companies, and enjoyed my bread puddings. But I wore my dark suit without nylons, and I knew there was something more.

Something more human, stories more personal and compelling. From Poetry for the People at Cal to Barbara Babcock at

Stanford, I knew the power of stories. Telling my own true story and helping others—like those accused and convicted of crimes—tell theirs became even more gripping as I worked for the faceless companies and sat in a fancy office. I missed the grit of prisons and the gravel of everyday lives filled with faults and family dramas.

| | | | |

I agreed to help Jake after his father Scott's almost desperate plea.

"It's just not right, what happened," he said.

They honestly hadn't understood. They had been sure the sentence was seven years.

As I dug into Jake's case, I found the transcript of a call he had with his mother.

"You fucked up, huh?" Jake's mother asked him in a recorded call to the jail after his arrest.

"Yep," Jake admitted.

"So, I mean, of course I don't know everything, but I know that it doesn't sound good."

"The dude's dead."

"That's what I heard."

"Yeah."

"That's . . . that's not good, baby."

"Nope."

"I mean, I know it wasn't intentional."

"No."

"But fuck, man. Didn't mean for that to happen, huh?" Mom asked.

"No."

"Yeah, fuck, that doesn't look good."

"I didn't even do nothing. I don't know what happened."

Trying to protect his mother from the truth, Jake didn't mention the knife.

"Uh-huh. Well, I'm glad you called. I was hoping you'd call and talk to me."

"Yeah."

"So, do you know anything about going to court or anything?"

"It's on Monday."

"Oh. So, well, I just—I, I don't know what to say, baby boy."

Silence.

"I hope it all turns out . . . something. I don't know."

I imagined his mother with the phone pressed hard against her ear. The recording reveals weeping, wishing he would say something instead of slipping away.

"All right."

"All right, baby?"

"Uh-huh."

"I love you."

"Love you, Mom."

I couldn't help but imagine my son Zach as a teenager calling me from jail to say that he had killed another person. I considered the pain from the overlooked perspective of the perpetrator's parents. The victim is the victim, after all, with all of the sympathy and outpouring of love and support. The killer's parents are left with unbearable shame and self-doubt. I would have to ask myself what I had done wrong, how my child could have done this. I would reassure myself that the death was not intentional, but still, there had been a fight and a knife and someone else's child was dead.

Jake Mendoza's file contained a picture of the victim, a young man. In Exhibit 1, he lay in the dirt and weeds on the side of a parking lot, near and slightly under a car. The left side of his face was darkened with blood and dirt. I wondered why he walked behind a car and not into the bar for help.

I felt slightly sick looking at the picture. This was a real kid—dark hair, jeans and a t-shirt, running shoes. He could have been any twenty-something at any bar. He could have been my son. Or yours.

The autopsy photos were even more explicit. There were three slashes from the knife. One in the young man's side was illuminated to show the depth. It was that cut, smaller than the doctor's thumb, that had caused the death. It was a simple, still photograph, but the reality of this young person's life having ended? That felt more gruesome than any episode of *Making a Murderer*.

Another trial exhibit showed the bar, the Happy Club. It had a short, flat roof and neon signs for Keystone, Budweiser, and Bud Light. Apparently happy hour was 5-7 pm. Above the door, a sign read, "If you drive your husband to drink . . ." I couldn't read the rest; I really wished I could.

I willed myself to turn my attention to the habeas petition I needed to write. Like a lot of these petitions, it would be based on a legal claim called "ineffective assistance of counsel." The Sixth Amendment to the US Constitution guarantees assistance of counsel. It says:

In all criminal prosecutions, the accused shall enjoy the right to a speedy and public trial, by an impartial jury of the State and district wherein the crime shall have been committed . . . and to be informed of the nature and cause of the accusation; to be confronted with the witnesses against him; to have compulsory process for obtaining witnesses in his favor, and to have the Assistance of Counsel for his defense.

In 1963, the US Supreme Court finally interpreted the last clause— "assistance of counsel for his defense"—to mean that attorneys should be provided to people who cannot afford them in all felony cases. *Gideon v. Wainwright* established that mere appointment of any old attorney does not satisfy the constitutional guarantee. Importantly, everyone has a right to reasonably competent representation.

Attorneys should do things like interview their clients, investigate videotapes that show someone other than the client confessing to the crime, consult with experts, and object when the prosecutor gets carried away—not to mention stay awake during the entire trial. Yet, attorneys have made these very mistakes and countless others. In *Strickland v. Washington*, the Supreme Court found that a defendant can obtain a reversal of his conviction or sentence if he can show that his attorney's performance fell below an objective standard and that, because of the deficient performance, there is a reasonable chance his results would have been different.

I argued that Jake's attorney should have explained that no good-time credits meant he would not be eligible for parole in seven years. If she had explained that crucial piece of information, Jake would not have pled guilty.

But the federal court could not conceive of Jake's misunderstanding, and the court denied our habeas petition. According to the court record, Ms. Thompson told the judge she needed to confirm that Jake would be eligible for parole in seven years. When she returned to court the next day, the federal court saw her explain that Jake would not receive good-time or work-time credits. The relationship between early parole and earning good-time credits was so obvious, so innately understood by the court, that it couldn't comprehend that Jake did not understand. The federal court found that Clara Thompson provided adequate legal assistance.

The federal court even used Scott's involvement in the first meeting as support for its rejection of Jake's claims: "The record shows that the trial court cleared the courtroom so that Petitioner, Counsel and Petitioner's father could confer regarding the possible plea." The court reasoned: "The presence and participation of Pe-

titioner's father undermines Petitioner's claim of 'heavy reliance'"
on Ms. Thompson and what she said or failed to say. As if Scott,
the owner of Scott's Auto Body in Humboldt, California, knew
enough about the legal system, sentencing statutes, and parole to
counsel his son on the consequences of a guilty plea.

I called Scott to tell him the news—that the habeas petition
was denied, and his son would likely spend the rest of his life
in prison.

I always tell my clients, and especially their parents, not to get
their hopes up. Still, denial takes your breath away.

"Oh . . ." he replied.

"I think we can appeal," I added to fill the silence that followed.

In law school, they don't train you what to say to someone
whose son has killed another young man. No one can imagine
telling a person, "Your son's life as you know it and as you dreamed
it is over." Offering the appeal sounded far better.

An appeal is false hope reduced to paper—especially an appeal
of a habeas petition. Between 1994 and 2004, federal appellate
courts decided 51,508 cases filed under the federal habeas statute
by state prisoners. Three hundred twenty-one of those prisoners
won. That is a success rate of 0.62 percent.[13] I spared Scott that
analysis. I told him the option was there. We had sixty days to ask
for permission to appeal.

"Thank you," he said. "I want you to know how much we
appreciate what you've done. We really are grateful for all your
hard work."

---

13 Blume, John H. "AEDPA: The "Hype" and the "Bite."" Cornell Law Faculty Publica-
tions, Paper 215, 2006.
http://scholarship.law.cornell.edu/facpub/215.

CHAPTER 8

IN FULL RESTRAINTS

On the surface, Deshaun and I shared almost nothing in common. I was a middle-aged mother of two living a privileged life of Gymboree and organic meals. I had struggled as a teenager at times, but I never got into real trouble and my mother provided serious stability.

Deshaun became my client when he was sixteen, but his delinquency career had started long before. He was a young African American who had smoked marijuana regularly since seventh grade. He often drank alcohol until he blacked out. Deshaun had a learning disability and some emotional problems. He had been a ward of the court since age fifteen. When he failed his probation because of poor behavior at school, he was taken from his mother's home and placed in a residential treatment center. He completed that program, but couldn't get off probation because he kept skipping school. When he took his mother's car twice without permission, he got removed from his home again.

I often thought of how my life could have looked more like Deshaun's. I could have been arrested for shoplifting, or "borrowing" my neighbor's Pinto to joy ride around Modesto with my other fourteen-year-old friends. Or both, ending up officially a "delinquent," with all of the terrible consequences that brings. I could have become pregnant my sophomore year in high school. I might have dropped out to hold a series of low-paying, dead-end jobs. Or I could have married a boyfriend I had in college and started a life of depressive episodes, re-enactments of my absent, mentally-ill father. Upon his eventual suicide, I would have become a widow and single mother.

I didn't. But I still felt connected to Deshaun.

Finally, he had gotten into real trouble. He'd taken a golf cart from Vacaville High School, and he and a buddy drove it to the market. Swearing and sagging, they strutted in. The buddy put some pills in his shirt; Deshaun shoved a bottle of Nyquil in his pants. If they drank the whole bottle, they knew they could get a little buzzed.

From the detailed record, the event was clear.

"I saw you guys take that stuff!" a store manager said.

A worn-out collared shirt reminded customers that he was an official of the Nugget Market. He walked up quickly to the boys, who were exiting the store, and he grabbed Deshaun's friend by the arm.

"Hella let go, man!" the friend yelled.

He started to pull away, and the manager pulled back. The friend flailed his elbows.

Another white man approached Deshaun. "Store security. You need to come back into the store."

"I didn't take anything," Deshaun said. "Don't touch me."

Suddenly, Deshaun was in a headlock.

Two young men ran up to help Deshaun, yelling something like, "Fuck, man, what the fuck you doing? We gonna fuck you up. Gonna call some other guys down here for back up. Fuck you up."

One of them pushed the friend and the manager to the sidewalk. They wrestled, grunting.

Pinned to the ground, Deshaun turned his head, trying to get more air.

"Hold still, you fucking punk." He spit on Deshaun and sat on top of him.

Another manager ran out through the glass doors. There was a chime, letting the Rockstar energy drinks and Trojans know they were unattended.

"Stay back. Stay out of this," the manager shouted at the growing group of kids.

"We're gonna beat your ass," someone yelled back.

Sirens wailed. The boys sprinted away, leaving Deshaun and his friend pinned against the concrete, two market employees on top of them. Twenty minutes passed before Deshaun was allowed to get up.

Deshaun was charged with felony second degree robbery. Robbery is the taking of something through force or fear. It's a much more serious charge than theft and could become one of three strikes on Deshaun's adult record. The force element, in this case, was Deshaun resisting the manager by turning his head in the headlock and struggling while he was thrown to the ground.

Deshaun went to trial. Since it was a juvenile case, there was no jury. He entered the courtroom in full restraints: legs shackled at the ankles by a system of locked cuffs and chains so he could only shuffle to the table near his attorney. Cuffs and chains also bound both arms to the chain around his waist. Iron restraints entirely constraining his person, all for stealing a bottle of Nyquil.

When his attorney objected, the judge agreed the chains were extreme.

"What hand do you write with, son?" the judge asked.

"Uh, my right hand, sir."

"Here's what we'll do. Bailiff, will you release his right hand so he can write? That way you can help with your defense."

"Yes, sir."

"The rest of the chains will stay on."

| | | | |

In New Orleans, I continued toiling at the Big Law firm while Doug continued playing for the Saints. The other lawyers from Louisiana took me in, taught me legal writing, fed me, and found amusement in my laid-back California voice and my quaint Left Coast politics.

I wasn't too surprised when I found out I was pregnant. I was pleased, even, and not too sad to cut down at work. Doug was excited about the pregnancy. He bought me CDs with music and stories in Spanish for the growing baby to hear in utero. He practiced his breathing coaching. He practiced his breathing. I ate a lot of corndogs.

About six months into the pregnancy, Doug decided we should get outdoors—go on a nature adventure, like we had in Berkeley.

"People don't go campin' 'round here," one teammate informed him with a chuckle.

Louisiana law allowed a 40-ounce piña colada cocktail in a Styrofoam cup with a straw from the cocktail drive-through as long as the driver did not actively drink it while driving, but unwritten law did not allow camping.

Always persistent, Doug convinced a teammate from Louisiana to tell us the "best" hiking spot around. The sparse trees and low hills reminded me of creepy witch movies. Still, we hiked alone in the woods and enjoyed the sunshine.

I was, however, largely pregnant, which meant I got winded easily, and I decided we should head back. After consulting the map, Doug found a simple shortcut to get me back to camp sooner.

Another hour passed, and the small, bare trees seemed to blend together. I was thirsty. Doug was panicking. It was not a great scenario.

Finally, we ran into another couple, and Doug asked them for directions and water. Concerned, the young hiker handed me her plastic water bottle without hesitation. Only after I felt revived did I realize how bad I'd been feeling. We thanked them and followed their directions back to the trailhead.

On the way, I realized that even in my state of thirst and pregnancy, I would not have asked strangers to help me. Doug hadn't hesitated. Step after step on that dusty path, grayish-green light surrounding us, I realized a fundamental truth: this man would take care of me and our child. We were going to be a family, and that felt solid and basic and right.

We spent the rest of the day at the campsite, enjoying the above-ground pool as if it were a five-star resort. Both of us were relieved to have dodged what felt like a risky situation. We didn't even mind the oppressive humidity and incessant bugs. This day-long adventure was our "babymoon."

Over the next few months, I grew huge and more nervous with each day. I worried our child would become a mass murderer or, more likely, a drug addict. I had no reason for such gloom, but I felt like I knew nothing about being a parent.

Far more urgent was the question of how I would get the baby out of my body. We had decided not to use any pain medication or epidural. We didn't want the baby to come out medicated, and Doug believed in my ability to handle pain. During labor, I screamed while he spoke calmly and led me in deep breathing. When I moaned, he massaged my aching back and brought me Dr. Pepper lip balm just to take my mind off of the pain for a second. Finally, baby Lillian arrived, and we cried together with relief and joy.

A few weeks later, the babymoon was over.

Between nursing and crying, I had been watching the Food Network non-stop with my mother, who had moved in for a few weeks to help with the baby. Sometimes we heard blurbs of news. I saw a special report about the Saints "kicking problems." I had no idea my husband was struggling.

As Doug walked through the door, I asked, "Babe, what is going on? Why didn't you tell me?"

"I didn't want you to get upset." He looked down.

I hadn't seen him in days. He slept upstairs with earplugs, needing real rest for grueling mid-season two-a-day training sessions, while my mom and I shared a queen bed in the baby's room. He must have eaten dinner with us and held the baby sometimes, but in my memory, he is blurred and at the edges.

"Yeah, I found out."

I couldn't keep the accusation from creeping into my voice. It was like I'd caught him sending a flirty email to a hot female trainer. I was sad he hadn't told me, and so tired and strung-out that I couldn't begin to be sympathetic. I was a Stanford-trained lawyer stuck in a small space with a tiny, irrational, endlessly needy creature and my mother. Mostly, suddenly, I felt angry.

"Just because I'm chained to this apartment doesn't mean I don't hear the news."

"I didn't want to stress you out."

"Stress me out?! I gave birth to your daughter with no drugs. She has barely slept for two minutes since we brought her home, and you think I can't handle it!"

"It just—it seems like you've been having a hard time."

No shit, I thought.

"You were so excited about this baby," I said, "and now that she's here and crying and not sleeping, it's like 'poof,' you disappear."

It was irrational, but I blamed it all on him.

My hard time soon became a nightmare entitled "Colic." Baby Lilli would start to cry at about noon; she didn't stop until around 10 pm, when she would crash for about an hour, maybe two.

I found if I held her tight against my chest and bounced her up and down, she could be soothed. I jogged endlessly up and down the stairs. I discovered she liked the sound of the hairdryer (that's how many different things I tried to get this kid to stop crying) and the bathroom fan, but only in a dark bathroom. Drenched in sweat and with extraordinary care, I would settle sleeping Lilli into the bassinet propped on the lid of the toilet. I would crawl to the couch and fall into a heap. But I felt no rest or triumph; only anxiety about how long she would sleep. Forty minutes was a good day.

A few brutal weeks later, I walked to the Superdome for the Saints playoff game. I carried Lilli in the Snugli close to my chest, my long, black coat around her. I was petrified. I had only taken a few quick trips to the grocery store, and I was embarrassed by her incessant crying. The whole world would know what a crappy mother I was, inept at soothing my child, totally incapable of knowing what was wrong. She scared me. She was inconsolable, inconsistent, unpredictable. And she was extremely loud.

Happily, so were the Saint fans. The Superdome was packed—72,000 people.

"Who let the dogs out?" blared the speakers.

"Who? Who, Who? Who, Who?" answered the rabid fans.

Only one other time in the history of the team had the Saints been in the first round of the playoffs. They weren't called the "Ain'ts" for nothing. Jim Haslett led a rag-tag group of players, crowned by superstar Ricki Williams (his dread-locked face adorned the entire city). My husband, with his impressive, come-back-from-baby, eleven straight field goals, had led the team to this game. Doug had solved his "kicking problem," and 72,000 people had come to witness him and the Saints make history for the team and the city.

I had put little purple earplugs in Lilli's ears. She was only six weeks old, and as bad as I was at mothering, I was determined not to completely screw up by rendering her deaf. But the noise, predictably, soothed my tyrant. Maybe she thought the cheering was for her. Even at one month, she loved attention.

The game dragged on. I left our seats in the family section and headed back to the VIP lounge. Looking back, I should have left the baby at home and had a couple of drinks with the wives, but I sat alone on the cheap, black leather sofa, watching the game on the big-screen TV and nursing Lilli. I didn't lift my head because I feared meeting someone's eyes or catching the attention of a drunk fan, some Cajun who had never heard of breastfeeding.

I didn't fit, a nervous mother in a Superdome bar. I didn't know how to be a mother, and I never felt at home in the NFL. Without my job to tether me to something bigger and with my husband consumed with his own work, I felt lost.

My sweater stuck to my back, and Lilli's dark hair clumped across her little forehead. We were hot and exhausted and embarrassed.

Finally, the Saints pulled ahead and won. New Orleans erupted with joyous drunken celebration. I guess Doug was happy. I'm not sure. All I knew was I wanted to crawl into a dark cave and sleep for a month. I wanted to take a shower, uninterrupted and long. I wanted a peaceful hike in the woods. I wanted to be free.

| | | | |

The idea of prison settled in the room like the stench of smoke. Doug, his partner Colin, and I sat in their company's expansive conference room overlooking Oakland's Lake Merritt. We worried in silence, staring at the lake and waiting. It was our first meeting with Doug's new attorney, Mike. We trusted Cris and the lawyer she had recommended. Mike specialized in federal cases, although I knew a good percent of those were drug cases.

Mike arrived, tall and lanky, suit and tie. *Only a few years older than us*, I thought. He seemed friendly as he shook our hands almost too eagerly for the situation.

"Wasn't this just a subpoena?" Doug wondered aloud as Mike told us about himself and the types of cases he had handled—he had begun to talk about plea bargains and trials in federal court.

"We have to think about the worst-case scenario," Mike responded.

Doug rolled his eyes. I could see him counting the dollar signs adding up somewhere above his head.

It is not an attorney's job to make clients feel better. We are not paid to say, "This will all blow over, don't worry about it." Part of the job is to give realistic expectations, maybe even worst-case scenarios. That way, any outcome seems like a success at best, inevitable at worst.

Doug knows this. He was, therefore, highly suspicious of the meeting. He knew he'd done nothing wrong—at least knowingly. My frugal husband thought the lawyers would try to make the risks of the subpoena seem more probable than they were, all so they could make him happy about spending thousands of dollars on legal bills. This was not a fun meeting.

The realities of the federal criminal justice system are incredibly grim. Over 90 percent of people charged with crimes plead guilty, whether they are or not. There is a huge incentive to do this: "Acceptance of responsibility" earns a defendant "points" in the federal sentencing scheme. In many cases, a few points could mean less years in prison, or the possibility of probation instead of incarceration. Pleading guilty avoids a lengthy trial, exorbitant legal fees, and prolonged uncertainty. A dragnet federal investigation like the one involving Doug's company could produce large numbers of charges, since the federal government knows its own "success rates." They simply charge everyone in sight, knowing most will fold and take pleas to avoid costly, risky trials.

Doug fumed. He hates distraction and delay and expense. He hates attorneys.

| | · | | |

The court appointed me as the attorney for the appeal of Nyquil-stealing, wrongly-shackled Deshaun. The fact that he never should have been shackled in court in front of the judge became our main point. During the trial, Deshaun's chains had forced him to shuffle up to the witness stand. There, he testified to his side of the story. He hadn't hit the manager; he had simply turned his head while struggling to get some air. Deshaun's whispered answers revealed his nervousness; his attorney had to ask him to speak up several times.

The judge found that Deshaun had committed robbery. Even though he had been in Juvenile Hall over eleven months, he was ordered to a residential youth facility, where he would live away from his family for an indefinite amount of time. He would be on probation for up to nine years.

The law says that adults cannot be shackled in a courtroom without a good reason. The judge must find compelling reasons to justify the use of chains—the maintenance of security, for instance. The courts have extended the prohibition to include stun belts as well, even though they cannot be seen by the jury. The courts believe the restraint impacts the defendant. It can preoccupy his thoughts, make it difficult for him to focus on the proceedings and his defense, and may impact his demeanor while testifying. One decision in Illinois had found shackling juveniles to be un-constitutional. There, the judge found, "wearing leg irons may seriously undermine a child's confidence in telling his side of the story, which would adversely affect the credibility determinations of even the most experienced juvenile judge."

Our judges in the Court of Appeal agreed. We won! They decided Deshaun should not have been shackled; that, in fact, no one should be shackled without good reason, least of all a child. This was a published decision, the new law of California.

One popular legal treatise later described the case, explaining what it meant and detailing why shackles should not be allowed:

[O]f concern is the potential unsettling effect on the defendant and therefore on his or her ability to present a defense, and the affront to human dignity, the disrespect for the entire judicial system which is incident to unjustifiable use of physical restraints, as well as the effect such restraints have upon a defendant's decision to take the stand.

So, sure, I freed all kids in California of the burden of being shackled without a good reason. But I also helped all juveniles present their defense and tell their stories. I bolstered respect for the entire judicial system. I defended human dignity! It was pretty damn cool.

But as I fought for the humanity that each of us has, even those accused of crimes, I felt overwhelmed with the avalanche of human demands that motherhood presented. I rarely left home because of Lilli's incessant crying. I felt isolated and frazzled by the consuming burden of nursing, the psychological defeat of sleeplessness.

While defending Deshaun, I had a small sense of what it was like to be trapped. I felt trapped as a mother. Still, I related to Deshaun, and I had a feeling the law could set me free, too.

CHAPTER 9

UNLUCKY

Christopher Brown and his buddy moved through the shush of the grocery store sliding doors that cold October night into the warmth of the store. Together, they strolled past the orange, red, and yellow bouquets in the floral section. His buddy called him "Lucky," but Christopher would soon see what an ill-fitting nickname that was.

They grabbed a cart and wandered down the first aisle. An employee approached them. They could tell he managed the place, because right under "R. Gonzalez," his shirt said, "Manager."

"How you doing?" the manager asked by the deodorant section.

"We're not stealing," Lucky's buddy said, annoyed.

"Nobody said you were. I just asked how you were doing." But the manager seemed interested in the high-priced items in the cart, like $7.00 razors.

"Well, we don't appreciate you and your employees harassing us." Christopher looked right into the manager's eyes.

"Have a nice day, then, fellas."

The manager walked toward the front of the store. But to be safe, he sent his security guard to follow them around.

"Manager told you to look at us?" Christopher's friend blurted out in anger.

"Okay. All right. Time for you two to get moving. Out of the store, now."

"We're not leaving. I'm tired of you guys following us," Christopher said.

While his friend said forget it and headed back to the sliding door and out into the night, Christopher gathered his razors, his whole milk, a couple boxes of mac and cheese, and a six pack of Bud and waited in the check-out line.

After paying, Christopher passed the manager and the guard standing shoulder to shoulder by the floral section, as if protecting the autumnal arrangements. Almost under his breath, Christopher whispered something. The manager later swore he had said something about going to the car and a gun and coming back. The guard was sure that Christopher said, "I have a gun in the glove compartment."

The two watched their customer pass through the doors, pass the big box of pumpkins, and put his bag of groceries into the trunk of an old Volvo. They didn't lock the doors to the store. They didn't know whether to believe what they thought they'd heard. But they did call the police. From inside the store, they watched the officers pull up, talk to Christopher's buddy for a second, then shout something at Christopher. The men watched "Lucky" jump into the Volvo and drive away.

Luck ran out for Christopher. The police caught him, and the jury convicted him of two counts of attempted criminal threats. The crimes were only "attempted" threats because the prosecution could not prove that the manager and the guard were in "sustained fear for their own safety." Since the guard and manager were not terribly scared, an actual criminal threat had not occurred. Still, Christopher's whispered words about a gun amounted to two felony convictions.

Taking on Christopher's appeal, I thought about the crazy things I had said in anger in my life. The standard, "I hate you!" in window-shattering volume to my mother during a teenage fight; the "I'm going to kill you!" to Doug for forgetting to pay the cable bill for so long that the collection agencies called and our TV was turned off; the "If you don't get quiet right this very minute, I am going to do something very bad to you," through clenched teeth in Lilli's ear as I squeezed my fingers around her upper arm, hard.

These are bad things to say. And I felt like I meant them, with every ounce of intent. I meant for them to instill fear and regret in my victims. Of course, I have never mentioned a gun or other weapons, and I knew my victims and they knew me. My mom and my husband and my kid did not fear for their lives. Because they did not have "sustained fear for their own safety," as the law requires, my angry outbursts would be only attempted criminal threats, like Christopher's.

For his attempted criminal threats, Christopher received felony convictions, a sentence of eight months in state prison, and two "strikes" on his record. His trial attorney had asked the judge to consider the convictions as misdemeanors rather than felonies. In warped reasoning, which I challenged in the appeal, the judge said he wouldn't consider the crimes misdemeanors because the law considered attempted criminal threats "serious" felonies and therefore strikes under the three-strikes law. What the judge didn't seem to see was that the crimes only became "serious" felonies when and because the judge determined that they were felonies rather than misdemeanors in the first place.

Wow, did this piss Lucky off. He had two strikes basically for saying "fuck off" to two grocery store employees who had harassed him for looking like he was going to steal $7.00 razors—that he didn't steal. With a history of petty crimes going back well into his teenage years, his third strike seemed inevitable. He was angry and desperately scared, and relying on me to relieve his panicked fury.

| | | | |

A sense of dread and panic crept into the conversation with our new lawyer, Mike, when we turned to finding another lawyer to represent Doug's partner, Colin. The three men looked to me to fill this desperate need. Colin needed his own attorney in case both he and Doug got charged with crimes and their "interests weren't aligned," a legal euphemism that filled me with anxiety. "Interests not aligning" would have looked like this: the feds breathing down Colin's neck, threatening twenty years in prison, and he decides to say anything to get himself and his family out of that—even saying that Doug knew about the collusion or that he must have known. Even though Doug could have done the same to Colin, Doug dealt more with Lance. The specter of Colin turning on Doug really freaked us out.

The next day, I spoke to another attorney friend, who suggested yet two more attorneys. One of the suggested attorneys was in Sacramento. Did every single attorney in the Bay Area have a conflict? One day, the glut of attorneys threatens the foundation of our country; the next, you would trade your first-born for someone who could take your case.

I met Doug and Colin at an Oakland restaurant to discuss options. Burger Gourmet served Philly cheesesteaks, steak sandwiches, and halal meat. Colin and Doug were the only customers. Their corner table was linoleum made to look like green marble; Colin's face was so pale that the dark circles stood out under his eyes. His shoulders slumped, making him look smaller than usual, even boyish. He and Doug both looked battered. No one hugged or smiled.

"How you holding up?" I asked.

"Okay I guess," Colin said.

After talking about attorney names, we all agreed we'd feel better if we could only get Cris to help. She had handled so many large white-collar federal investigations. She specialized in managing the investigation so it didn't turn into criminal charges. But we didn't have Cris. Doug had Mike. Colin had no one. The worst-case scenario pervaded our table like the smell of grease.

"Do you want to order something?" Colin looked up for the waitress.

"Not hungry," I said.

The men, dedicated coffee and beer drinkers, partakers of the Negroni or a Manhattan, both had cups of tea.

| | | | |

As depressing and tedious as it was, after baby Lilli had mostly stopped crying, I returned to my work at the Big Firm. I had become the kind of lawyer people hate: reviewing documents for days on end, charging $300 per hour, defending the neurological-disorder-causing toxin producers, the companies that make Big Tobacco look like the cute neighbor girl selling baked goods.

Before baby Lilli could even sit up, Doug got a call from his agent: the Saints were "letting him go." Doug had helped them win their first playoff game in franchise history. He'd been with the team for seven seasons and had been named alternate to the Pro-Bowl twice. He had one of the highest field goal percentages in NFL history. Still, at thirty, he was ancient.

"Let's go home," Doug said. "Let's just get out of here."

"What about my job?"

"You don't care about that job," he said.

He was right in a way; I didn't love that job. But the prospect of leaving it—my colleagues, my reason to shower in the morning—flooded me with uncertainty.

Maybe he hadn't noticed how quiet I'd become when he said, "I'm going to get another job pretty fast. Remember when the 'Niners cut me? It only took a few weeks. It'll be good to be back in the Bay Area. Our people are there."

I *did* want to see my friends. I needed someone to talk to, and I was desperate for help with this baby. But more than that, I was just tired. I didn't have the energy to push back against Doug and his determination. Without considering the consequences of selling our home and quitting my job, Doug put our condo on the market, I gave notice, and we hightailed it out of New Orleans forty-five days later.

Weeks in California turned to months. No teams needed an old kicker. It became apparent that my acquiescence to Doug's decision was a colossal mistake. It was like taking that third tequila shot, or getting that tattoo on your lower back one day in the '90s—a decent-seeming decision at the time, but hindsight illuminates how much it sucked. I had followed other men around as a teenager to near-disastrous results. Now, there I was, even as an adult, following a man blindly, against my own interests and sanity, away from professional development and intellectual challenge, toward what ended up being the Burrito Tour of Merced.

We stayed with my mother-in-law for six weeks. I pushed Lilli in the stroller in 100-degree heat through the newly-built east area of Danville, past the stucco houses all painted a similar shade of peach, twig-like trees planted precisely down the mow strip. My mother-in-law happily watched Lilli babbling in the kitchen and stacking blocks on the floor and annoying Bailey the dog, but nights were still long. I didn't see all the friends I had been missing. They lived an hour away in the city, hanging in Golden Gate Park reading the Sunday newspaper, working as childless lawyers at the prestigious firms of San Francisco and Silicon Valley. They were starting their own non-profits helping the disadvantaged youth of East Palo Alto.

Doug must have been there at times, but in my memory, I spent six weeks alone on my mother-in-law's new micro-suede sofa watching Lilli play on the floor. I caught five-minute naps out of boredom. I crumbled into myself with loneliness. Intellectually, I understood that Doug was stressed about staying in shape and finding a new job to support his new family, but he might as well have been kicking balls over the Eifel Tower or lifting weights in China. He just wasn't there.

When Doug still had no job two months later, we moved on to my mom's. The heat in Merced was similar—excruciating, stifling, exhausting—but at least my mom had a pool and trees that had grown tall enough to offer some shade. These were the six weeks of the Burrito Tour. The Central Valley in those days lacked any real restaurants. No Applebee's. Not even a Chevy's. There was no shortage of burrito shops, though, and Doug and I decided we would try every burrito in town.

Fascinated that a certain chicken burrito only cost $2.70, I asked, "What comes on it?"

"Cheeken," said the guy behind the drive-through window. It was too hot to park and walk across the asphalt of the parking lot in the blazing sun.

"Chicken. Anything else?" I ask.

"Cheeken. Just cheeken."

"I'll take two."

Despite what I might have thought, crowning the "Best Burrito in Merced" was not actually our low point.

A friend had a vacant condo in San Diego that we could rent cheap. Needing space, independence, and some semblance of adulthood, we committed to six weeks there. We strapped the

Mega Saucer (a primary-colored, plastic monstrosity of a toy/walker) to the top of our SUV and set off.

Doug worked out with a strangely large group of unemployed NFL kickers living in the San Diego area. He meditated, called his agent, and worked out for a second time; he didn't hang around the apartment much. After I had taken endless walks alone on the beach—broken up by a smattering of grocery shopping and grinding my own baby food—I had to do something.

I started by registering for the California Bar Exam. It felt good to have something on the calendar, even if it was four months away. Lilli was nine months old; she had slept through the night about three times.

I felt listless and weak. I went to the OBGYN because my body felt strange and bloated. I left the office crying and with a reason for my exhaustion and aching breasts: I was pregnant.

I called Susie, my best friend from college. While I sat on the edge of the tub in our shitty rental, I could imagine her single life in the city, working for a tech company, living in a bay-windowed apartment with views of the pyramid and Coit Tower.

"Wow," she said.

"No shit," I said through tears.

"Hon. What are you going to do?"

"I don't know. I mean. I signed up to take the Bar. I have to do something with my life. I'm going to be out to here," I held my hands two feet in front of my belly, though I knew she couldn't see. "How can I study with pregnant brain? Oh my God. What if I fail?"

"You can do it. You are a strong, powerful mama!"

"I mash up vegetables and change shitty diapers for a living. Before that, I cut and pasted Word documents. I haven't slept in almost a year, and this blouse was on the clearance rack at Target."

Despite Susie's pep talk, studying for the California Bar was endless, excruciating drudgery. The Louisiana Bar was notoriously easy—the questions on the business law section repeated every year. Everyone said I had to take a review course to even have a chance to pass in California. I had graduated from one of the best law schools in the country and spent over $100,000 doing it, but felt entirely unprepared to pass the Bar.

So began that winter. After pulling myself out of bed and spreading some Cheerios on the highchair so I could get dressed, I would leave Lilli at the home daycare in Walnut Creek and schlep to the conference room on the second floor of a beige office building next to Target. Armed with snacks to stave off the feeling of starvation that was just pregnancy, I sat with a room full of other students and watched videos of a guy telling us what constitutes a will and who qualifies as an intestate heir. After six hours of class, I would go to a café, order a decaf vanilla latte, and pretend to study community property and contracts while mostly I watched life go by. I had to be home by five. Dinner, bath for Lilli, bedtime stories and practice exams, three or four made-up fact patterns that I outlined, then wrote the answers to longhand.

Repeat. Repeat and repeat and repeat, every day until the exam. I was desperate to pass.

Months later, I typed my Social Security Number into the Bar's website and read: "Your name does not appear on the pass list."

Feeling myself begin to sink, I entered my number a second time.

Again: "Your name does not appear on the pass list."

It felt like I entered those nine digits another twenty-seven times. Twenty-seven more times, the computer told me, "You are a fat pregnant lady with baby brain. You did not, nor will you ever, pass the California Bar Exam."

Doug and I had plans to spend a couple days in Carmel with friends. I cried all the way there and all the way home. I was sure I would never take the Bar again. Lilli was seventeen months old. In two months, right before the July Bar, I would give birth to our second child. I couldn't re-take the exam with a newborn. Passing statistics are bad enough—only 50 to 60 percent of people pass their first time. Once failed, pass rates plummet to around 20 percent. Demoralized, I thought maybe I could take it when the kids were in school.

Desperate hope made me check again first thing that next Monday morning. The State Bar publishes the pass list on Mondays. Anyone can see who has passed, this time by name, not just number. I scrolled down to the B's.

And there it was: Shanti Brien.

Holy shit. There was my name! I was ecstatic. And I was pissed. I was a very-pregnant woman who had suffered what felt like a major injustice. I was *pissed*.

"State Bar of California," answered an unassuming telephone receptionist.

"Hi. My name is Shanti Brien. On Friday, I typed my number into the website and nothing came up. Today, my name is on the pass list."

"Ok . . ." she said slowly—as if there were no problem at all.

"Can you check to make sure I passed?"

After a few seconds, she confirmed that I had indeed passed. "Congratulations."

"I don't think you understand. Do you realize the kind of weekend I've had? I am seven months pregnant. I have gained more than forty pounds—already! I'm miserable. I cried all weekend. I thought I would never pass. Ever."

"Well. I'm sorry?"

"Sorry?! This was massive infliction of emotional distress."

"Ma'am. Mistakes happen."

Little consolation, I thought, as I fell into a chair and considered the first beer of my pregnancy—even if it was nine in the morning. There was clearly no apology forthcoming, no one concerned for the health of my unborn child, no one invested in my mental health—which was clearly deteriorating. It felt like an ominous welcome to my legal career in California, a career of helping people and even saving people, the career I had dreamt about for so many years.

| | | | |

With credit for time spent in jail, "Lucky" Christopher Brown—wrongly suspected non-thief of razors—got out of prison pretty early in our appeal process. A former inmate out of custody, freaking out and with access to a phone? He was in constant contact with his attorney—me.

"Well, hello, Attorney Shanti Brien. Obviously, you are too busy to answer my call. I tried you an hour ago, and you didn't answer then, either. I'm really getting pissed off about your unresponsiveness. I need to talk to you."

Each time he couldn't reach me right away, he seemed more and more infuriated.

"You said the other side was supposed to file his brief or some shit last week, and I have not heard word one from you. You're out of town? You think other cases are more important? You obviously don't understand. I have two fucking strikes. I am going to go to prison for the rest of my fucking life if you do not do something about this."

I listened in shock. Never had a client spoken to me in that way. Normally, they appreciated my dedication. Not Christopher.

"I got a letter from you the other day? Fucking thing had chocolate on it. I swear to God it did. You are the absolute worst attorney I have ever had. Totally fucking incompetent. I'm calling the State Bar on you."

Christopher seemed like he had studied the law almost as thoroughly as I had studied for the California Bar. He had specific complaints about the legal issues I argued in the appeal. He sent me the names of cases I should read and why they supported his arguments. I imagined him in the county law library day and night.

The legal input was excessive, but fine. It was the tone of the voicemails that crossed the line—the swearing and the personal attacks. Almost every week, if I couldn't answer his call as it came through, he would vomit a stream of complaints and obscenities into my voicemail.

One day, he called me four times in a row. He left a message with a new address to mail letters. I pressed redial to confirm the address with him. When Christopher answered and heard my voice, he exploded. How dare I disrespect his privacy by calling him? What kind of incompetence was he dealing with?

"I won't do this," he yelled. "I don't know what I will do if you don't get this right. I might have to run off to Mexico. I might have to do something very bad."

I listened because I wanted to answer his questions and respond to his concerns. I wanted to help him, and he needed help. But he was angry and threatening, and his words hurt.

Still, I did my job. I argued in his appeal that the judge should have instructed the jury that the victim's fear needed to be reasonable. I also argued that the trial judge misunderstood his discretion, believing he could not sentence the conviction as a misdemeanor.

Ultimately, my arguments did not sway the appellate court. Christopher's convictions for criminal threats were upheld—we lost his case.

For the first and only time, I was not upset to lose an appeal. He had written me twenty-seven letters (three in one day). I lost track of the number of harassing calls. He convinced me that his words could evoke an emotional reaction from his victims—a deep-in-the-belly fear—and that, even worse, he might act on those fearful, angry words. His threatening calls and letters all but convinced me that he was guilty of making criminal threats.

This did not matter to his appeal. I don't think my emotions had a bearing on the way I carried out my professional obligations to my client. I argued intelligently and with all my resources that the judge should have considered Christopher's attempted criminal threats as misdemeanors, not felonies, which had nothing to do with guilt or innocence. But I had come to believe that Christopher "Lucky" Brown was guilty of scaring undeserving people, people simply trying to do their jobs. And that mattered to me.

Still, if I am entirely honest with myself, I can't help but think that I did not do my very best as his attorney. He threatened my sense of professionalism and my personal boundaries. He touched my insecurities about being a woman and a lawyer. He got to me.

I had studied and fought so hard to become an attorney in California and to become a certain type of attorney—caring, generous, professional, helpful—to a certain type of client—struggling, ill, forgotten, broken. Now that I had become that attorney for those people, I felt overwhelmed. If I had taken the time to listen to Christopher and his complaints, I would have heard foreboding whispers of failures to come.

CHAPTER 10

MALPRACTICE

"We've decided to go ahead and appeal."
Scott Mendoza was calling from his auto body shop. He wanted to continue fighting for the son who took the plea bargain neither of them had understood.

"This is what Jake wants?" I asked.

"Absolutely. He feels bad asking me and his mother to pay for it all"—Scott was being honest—"but we have it together, and we want you to do it."

I reminded him that the appeal was not automatically allowed. In federal habeas cases, a criminal defendant has to ask the court to allow an appeal.

"Yeah, I know. But it seems like our last shot."

Last shot, maybe. But also the beginning of a long road that might lead to a dead end.

Still, I was glad to think that the Mendozas were fighting a little harder for justice, and I was happy to play my part as I sat down to write up the notice of appeal.

I carved out an hour, planning to finish before meeting a friend from law school. I opened *Federal Rules of Civil Procedure*—the rules by which the federal courts run—and turned to "Notices of Appeal." There, I encountered Rule 4:

(A) In a civil case . . . the notice of appeal required by Rule 3 must be filed with the district clerk within 30 days after entry of the judgment or order appealed from.

Thirty days! I had told Scott we had sixty. Sixty days is the deadline for appealing in *state* court, not federal.

Frantic, I scanned the page for exceptions. Our case met none of them. I had missed the deadline.

I called Christy, a criminal defense attorney and a good friend. I needed advice.

"Oh my God. Christy. I—" I couldn't even put the words together. "I screwed up. I don't even know how. I told a client the wrong date. They trusted me. This kid is twenty. They fed him a plea he didn't understand, and he's looking at fifteen-to-life." I pictured the father and son from the photo, arms tight around each other. "How can I possibly tell them?"

"Wait. What happened?" Christy said. "You missed a deadline?"

"A Notice of Appeal." I had started crying. Jake Mendoza was sitting in a prison cell, Scott at home, both thinking I could offer freedom when my mistake meant I could offer them nothing at all. "I didn't file it when I needed to."

It was the worst mistake of my career. It would unmoor me almost as much as Doug's mistakes in the waning days of his football career.

| | | | |

Like a good wife and mother of two tiny children, I followed Doug from our third California rental to Minneapolis when the Vikings picked him up after the season of wandering around the state had passed.

If I had been afraid to bring baby Lilli to the Superdome, I now had a toddler and a newborn in the Metrodome. The Vikings tried to make it easier for the players' families by having babysitting at the stadium. What they didn't understand was that I needed help taking a shower, shaving my legs, finding the favorite teething toy—all before getting from our apartment into the elevator, through a strange city into a packed stadium.

Of course I understood that Doug wanted his family to be with him. Together, Doug and I had built the family who could do it all! Just like he and I could swim and kayak and hike and canoe our way through our adventure honeymoon, we could power through an NFL game with a couple of babies. He literally said things like, "Won't it be fun?" And though I might have wanted to smack him for not understanding how hard it would be, I couldn't resist his boundless optimism, and I liked the idea of our girls, even though they were both under two, having some sense of what their father did. So, I dressed up somewhat in jeans, boots, and a nice sweater, packed up the double stroller, the diapers and the binkies, strapped on my nursing bra, and inched through traffic to the stadium. I dropped the kids at the childcare and sat in the family section.

The game was close but seemed to drag on. Usually, when a score was within three points, I would start to feel nervous, but the Vikings were behind by six, so Doug wouldn't have to attempt the kind of game-winning field goal that made me nauseous. What made me anxious now was the idea of being far from my babies. With five minutes left in the fourth quarter, I decided to beat the rush of the crowd, pick up the girls in the babysitting room, and watch the end in the family lounge.

On the way, I heard the roar of the Vikings scoring a last-minute touchdown.

Great, I thought, *Doug will come out on the field, kick the extra point*—an act as natural to him as brushing his teeth—*and they'll win by one point, even without a field goal.* I wouldn't have to vomit in front of the other ladies.

But Doug missed the extra point. I couldn't remember him doing that. Ever. Extra points are gimmes. All of America knows the kicker will make it through the goalposts.

Without the extra point, the game was tied. It was a huge mistake. And it was Doug's. I knew that for at least a week, he would be quiet and withdrawn. My already tense home life would be tinged with gloom.

As the game moved into the final minutes, I hoped that he would get the chance to kick the game-winning field goal. Given that chance, he might redeem himself.

I had actually seen the missed extra-point kick from the family lounge. It was broadcast on a large-screen TV set up for us to watch the post-game show. Wives and mothers had glanced up quickly as I walked in, loaded with Ceci in the front pack, diaper bag on my shoulder, and Lilli dragging behind. The room was quiet except for the TV announcers blaring Vikings' overtime statistics. The game was tied and would go into overtime.

Lilli had been cooped up all day and bounced around the room, crazed from sleep-deprived hyperactivity. I bribed her with cookies just to sit still. No other families seemed to have little kids (or they had left them home). How could I have been so stupid, so eager to please Doug that I had brought our babies to this place? People drank heavily but quietly; someone chain-smoked in a corner. Lilli screamed and jumped, trying to escape my hand, her chair, the room. Ceci started crying from hunger, and I jiggled her while running after Lilli. Soon her cries were constant, roaring over the TV. I needed to feed her, but there was nothing that would make Lilli sit. Not watching her father on the big-screen TV, not watching him miss a *second* extra point.

It seemed impossible, but no matter how long I stared at the television with my screaming girls on me, I couldn't change what had happened: Doug missed the second extra point. The Vikings lost.

Women in black leather and lacquered fingernails stared at me. Was it the screaming children or the flailing husband who'd just joined the team? All I knew was I had to get out of that smoky, horrible, dark place.

Five, then ten, then fifteen eternal minutes passed in the family area as I ran behind Lilli, pleading for her to sit still so I could feed Ceci. I had no one to ask to hold her, nowhere to breastfeed privately. Ceci wailed. Time seemed to expand, but I knew we would be no better off in the teeming walkways or parking lots. Sweat poured down my back. Breast milk leaked through my nursing bra, through my shirt, and onto the Bjorn. I was sticky and reeked of milk.

Finally, sure that Doug would be ready to meet us, I pushed my way out of the family room, forcing Lilli into the tunnel along with the crowd that had lined up, waiting for the players to come out of the locker room.

What seemed like hours later (but was really minutes), Doug appeared in the tunnel. He had showered and wore civilian clothes, which made him seem smaller than he'd been on the field. With his head down, he walked quickly toward the car; I followed. When he got in the front, I got in the back where I could nurse Ceci. I started to cry.

I knew it was insensitive, knew that Doug was having a terrible time, but I couldn't seem to help myself: "Where were you!?"

"I was in the locker room, Shanti." His voice was flat, angry.

"We were waiting. It took you so long. The baby is so hungry."

"I hear that."

"Well?"

Our eyes connected in the rear-view mirror.

"There were reporters and . . ."

Of course, Doug was dealing with his own hell, one that would be on sports radio shows and headlines for days.

"Babe. What happened?" I asked.

"What do you mean? I missed two PATs. Didn't you see?"

"I mean, how did that happen?" Maybe there was an explanation that made sense—a strained groin or a sudden onset of the flu.

"I don't know, Shant. It happened."

In her car seat, Lilli started crying too.

I knew this wasn't the best timing, but I couldn't seem to think beyond the force of Lilli's cries, the heat of Ceci's desperate, helpless body too close to mine, the noise of screaming drunken fans passing our SUV. I took on Doug's failure as my own. He wouldn't cry or scream, so I took the intensity of the emotions and the stress and flung them back at Doug in anger.

"This is all too much for me. I can't begin to do it right. Be your wife, be a good mom. I don't know if I can come to any-more games."

I wanted it all to go away. All of it.

"Aren't you being a little dramatic?"

"You have no idea what it was like in there with Ceci scream-ing and Lilli running wild." Knowing I was acting irrationally and even feeling like I might regret it, I said, "That might have been the hardest day of my life."

He shoved the key into the ignition and pulled us out of the lot. No one said a word during the twenty-minute ride home.

The Vikings cut him a few weeks later. I was sure our days in the NFL were over. I was too overwhelmed by my two babies to get a real sense of how Doug felt about that—relief or regret or some mix of failure and utter release, he never told me—but I was sure that I did not feel sad.

| | | | |

"God," I said to Christy, "I have to make this right for the Mendozas."

Tears rolled down my face. I had not been so scared or cried so much since the weekend I was sure I had failed the biggest exam of my life and would never practice law in California. I hadn't faced such a sense of failure and such an insatiable urge to run away from it since the Vikings game.

When Christy called me back, she asked if I wanted to talk to Ted (who happened to be a law partner with Cris, the white-collar crime expert, though this was years before Doug and I would want her to handle our case). Ted and Cris and their firm were some of the best, possibly the very best criminal defense attorneys in the Bay Area and California at large.

For a moment, I thought, *No, this is too embarrassing.* How could I admit to a well-respected attorney—obviously better than me—that I missed such a simple and important deadline? But I thought of the Mendozas and the fact that I had to try to undo the mess. If there was any possible way to fix the situation, I needed to know.

While Christy contacted Ted, I did some research myself. Deep in the small print, I found that Rule 4 does allow an attorney to ask (I would beg! I would plead!) for an extension of time to file the Notice of Appeal. The "motion" must be made within thirty days of the deadline, and the attorney must show "excusable neglect or good cause."

In my mind, the mistake was inexcusable. But so much of the law has to do with interpretation of language. I was within the thirty days of the deadline. I needed to present the court with a good reason for my mistake. Even then, it would be up to the judge to decide whether to grant my request or not.

There was also—horrifyingly—the issue of malpractice. I didn't research it then, but it creeped into the shadows of my growing panic. I suspected that missing deadlines was at the top of the list of legal malpractice claims. In fact, failure to know a deadline, failure to file a document, and failure to calendar a deadline, all lead the list of formal complaints against attorneys. I had failed to know the right deadline, failed to put it on my calendar, *and* failed to file the document.

Still, I didn't have time to worry about malpractice. The Mendozas' last attorney had failed them by giving them the wrong advice, and I meant to fix that problem, not compound it.

I called Ted later that afternoon, my voice hoarse and worn from crying. He gave me solid advice—legal advice about which cases to include in the brief—but more importantly, he made me feel a little better: "This happens to great lawyers. This happens *all the time.*"

"But listen," he said (and I will never forget this), "you do not need to apologize to the father."

"I let them down," I argued.

"Tell him you are doing your best to get it fixed. That's all you need to do."

I dreaded making the call, but forced myself to dial before the kids were home from school, before Doug was back from work, before I could decide it had gotten too late in the day for a professional call.

The minute I heard Scott's kind voice saying, "Ms. Brien. How are you?" I jumped in before the crying could overtake me again.

"Do you remember me telling you that the deadline for filing the notice of appeal was sixty days?"

He remembered.

"I made a mistake. The deadline was thirty days. That was last week." I just said it, no apology.

"Well, I have to tell you, I am not surprised." His voice was quiet. "Disappointed, maybe, but not surprised. That's just how this mess seems to be going."

I felt myself relax. Scott Mendoza was one kind, unbegrudging, charitable man. With a flash, I recognized my own petty, selfish, immature past: my ingratitude to my mother for making turkey loaf; my holier-than-thou attitude at the big New Orleans law firm; my anger at the State Bar for their minor, two-day mistake. Maybe most horribly, Scott Mendoza's grace made me regret my insensitivity to Doug's career challenges. He had worked his ass off for me and our growing family. The media amplified his mistakes and shortcomings, and I had provided no empathy at all. In fact, I'd resented Doug for my stress with the kids and for my unhappiness.

Scott could have been angry to the point of a malpractice lawsuit. Scott could have screamed at me and pointed out that I had extinguished his family's last hopes. He didn't. He was just sad and disappointed, and I fully understood.

I told him there was a way, under the court's rules, to ask for an extension of the deadline, even when the deadline had passed. "I've been preparing that motion and will file it today."

I didn't explain my excuses to Scott, but to the court, I detailed the nightmare I had been living, which—once I had listed it on paper—didn't seem even remotely exaggerated. First, there were Lilli's strange childhood illnesses. Flat warts (I had never even heard of flat warts) covered her chin and required endless trips to the dermatologist. She had a lazy eye that required a patch several hours each day. She had a developed an obsession with licking her fingertips, which led to some crazy diseases. Like pin worms.

"Mom, come check out my poop!" ten-year-old Lilli yelled. "It's moving!"

Part of my argument in the brief was that when all three of these issues emerged within the same week, any attorney could miss a deadline.

As if Lilli's ailments weren't enough, Doug and I suspected Ceci had Obsessive Compulsive Disorder. She had been having crying fits, unusually passionate ones, over the way a sock fit or a missing rainbow tutu. It had gotten to the point where she could hardly get dressed in the mornings without hours of streaming tears and begging for help, only to refuse any suggestions or assistance, followed by me screaming and forcing her into the car in her pajamas.

On top of all this, our youngest had just turned two. An active, energetic toddler was enough to drive someone to the brink.

And my three kids were just finishing up their third round of head lice.

The day I shoved Ceci in the car screaming, then later forgot a dermatology appointment, all with a squirming, fussy toddler on my hip? That was the day I was supposed to have filed the notice of Jake Mendoza's appeal.

I wrote to the court about my kids.

I wrote them about "Lucky" Christopher Brown's unnerving voicemail messages and harassing letters.

I admitted to the court I was reconsidering my career as a lawyer.

When I wrote those words in the brief, I realized for the first time that they were true. I had dreamed of being a lawyer since high school, when I'd acted as an attorney on the mock trial team and did pretty damn well. I'd become even more sure when I first watched *LA Law* with my mother at fifteen. I'd wanted to be a lawyer so much that when I gave it up for Doug's career, feelings of inadequacy and uncertainty overwhelmed me, made me a bad mom, and threatened my marriage. But in the face of my kids' needs, my failure in the Mendoza case, and the endless defeats I had faced as an attorney and a mom and a wife, I was convinced I could not handle it all.

Writing the brief, I realized that the passion, even the mere attention I gave to my clients, had waned. When I stepped back, I realized I didn't actually want to face the ugly mess that every single case presented: plea bargains and life-ending sentences forced upon young people, guilty and not. I fought so hard for minute victories that did not seem to matter, while most cases ended in losses, injustice that was utterly maddening. Family life was a morass; the criminal justice system a cesspool. I was drowning in both.

CHAPTER 11

♀

AIDING AND ABETTING

S tanding in the long, marble hallway of the Ninth Circuit
Court of Appeal with Nick Yang's small, Hmong mother
and her two, young companions, I thought on the fact
that Nick sat in prison, serving a seventy-two-year-to-life sentence for driving to the park where his passenger shot and killed
two people. These three women and I stood in the second-most
intimidating court in the country. (The next stop would be the
US Supreme Court, but it takes so few cases that only a handful
of attorneys ever argue there.) So even after almost ten years of
representing people in their appeals, the magnitude of this predicament, the knowledge that I was Nick's last real chance, and
the sheer, echoey massiveness of the courtrooms made the Ninth
Circuit just plain scary.

Still in the hallway, I spoke softly and told Nick's mother and
sister about the procedures and what to expect in court. It was
my standard opening. The sister was her mother's translator. They
knew that Nick would not be in the courtroom. I explained that

the mother and the sister would not be able to say anything to the judges either.

The mother looked up with bewilderment and sadness. She began to cry.

"My baby. Please help my baby."

. I felt pressure at the back of my eyes. I thought of Nick, locked in a small, dark cage for the rest of his life.

| | | | |

"Babe. Are you . . . ?"

I stood in the doorway; the shades of our bedroom were drawn, and the room was thick with sleep and sweat. Doug didn't roll over. He just lay there, still, the gray in his black hair standing out against the white of the sheets.

A few days had passed since our meeting with our lawyer, Mike. We hired him to respond to the subpoena and to handle the unknown and unspoken "whatever might happen after that." We still had not secured a lawyer for Colin, and I carried the weight of that worry as I moved through soccer games, baking chicken nuggets, and shoe shopping for growing feet.

The afternoon I walked into the bedroom, Doug and I had planned on going to a fundraising event in San Francisco for our good friend Suzanne's non-profit. She helped low-income and at-risk kids get to college by teaching them entrepreneurship. Doug loved the organization—the can-do-through-hard-work spirit of it. He was a guest of honor as a sponsor of the event. We would sit with Suzanne and her husband at their table. It would be a great chance to get out, have a few cocktails, and try to forget about the whole situation.

"I can't get up," Doug said slowly.

I walked to the side of the bed and looked down on him. "What do you mean? It's Suzanne's big night. You're a sponsor."

"I can't go."

"We have to. You can't cancel two hours before."

"I already did."

"You—"

"I told her I was sick."

"Are you?"

"I feel . . ." His face contorted.

I was sure he had a terrible headache, the sudden pain of it overwhelming. Then, I realized that my husband was crying. I had seen him suffocating in this kind of gloom only once before, when his dad died suddenly and unexpectedly at age fifty-one.

Doug was simply not a man who had legal problems. He had been through career slumps: cut from the 49ers in his second year, cut from the Saints even after becoming one of the league's most accurate kickers, cut from the Vikings only a few months into the season. But he hadn't been grounded often by his parents and was never in trouble at his strict Catholic high school. In college, he raised hundreds of thousands of dollars for Big Brothers Big Sisters, and though he'd had a few speeding tickets over the years, he had never, like me, done so much as cheated on a history test in ninth grade. He had never gone on shoplifting sprees or befriended Costa Rican drug dealers. Since the day I'd met him, when he was twenty-two years old, he had moved through the world with enormous integrity. He never took for granted what the NFL gave him: the money, the recognition, the role-model status. But even if he'd done nothing wrong, I knew he thought that the suggestion of involvement with Lance could bring down everything he'd built.

It was the idea of all his good, hard work being for naught that had him in our bed that day, curtains drawn, crying. He was faced with admitting that he had done something wrong, something criminal—even if he hadn't been aware he was doing it. He might be facing a prolonged trial that might send him to prison. He was faced with the choice of fighting the charges and risking a long prison sentence, or pleading guilty and admitting to crimes he did not commit. Having a choice almost seemed to make things worse.

But for me, as the man's wife, as a mother, and a girl who grew up without a father, I couldn't conceive of a single crime that he should not plead guilty to if it meant he would be home.

I sat on the edge of the bed but couldn't quite touch him. It was his decision. I had such strong feelings, but he already knew my thoughts. He was the one facing humiliation, censure, even a prison cell. But I felt utterly terrified too. Suddenly, the room felt too close, the decision too big.

| | | | |

When Nick's case was called, I moved directly to the podium, only feet from the elevated, giant desk—the "bench"—where the three, old, white men adorned in black loomed over me. Like the hallway, the courtroom was all marble, reminding me of the Big Firm in New Orleans—home to the good ol' boys and a place where I clearly didn't fit. The three gray-headed giants—intellectually, professionally, and in sheer number of years my superiors—stared, waiting for me to begin. Nothing about them reflected the urgency of the fact that they would now decide Nick Yang's future. Rather, they sat patiently, even slightly bored looking. Maybe it was something in their expressions, in their maleness, that made me feel the same self-doubt, the nervousness my five-year-old self had facing the man dressed as a terrible sad clown in my grandparents' chilled living room.

I felt the eyes of the audience at my back as I arranged my notes and told myself to take a moment and breathe. Still, I knew the courtroom could hear the tremor of my first words as I said into the small microphone, "This case arises at the intersection of several clearly established principles."

Wanting to emphasize how the United States Supreme Court's prior decisions clearly prohibited what the prosecutor had done, I explained: "The prosecutor's scheme to exclude from the jury's consideration two important witnesses put such duress on them as to prevent them from making a free and voluntary choice of whether to testify or not. This principle was established in *Webb v. Texas.*"

I was partial to this case, one that felt lucky in part because it was decided in 1972, the year I was born.

A dry beginning, maybe, but before I could really get going, one judge interrupted me. This wasn't uncommon, and I actually felt relieved to address his concerns head on.

He asked if the prosecutor's offer of plea bargains in exchange for silence wasn't "a commonplace understanding, both written and non-written?"

I jumped on my chance to point out that the California Court of Appeal actually declared this exact practice unconstitutional in *People v. Treadway,* "Which occurred, unfortunately, after Mr. Yang was convicted without the benefit of the exculpatory testimony."

Another judge jumped in, pointing out that the California court had already decided Nick's case, finding that it did not matter whether the prosecutor's plea-bargaining scheme was unconstitutional or not. The California court found that Nick had "failed to show prejudice," meaning that the witnesses' statements were not reasonably likely to change the outcome of the trial because the evidence still showed Nick's "accomplice liability for the crimes." We were back to the aiding and abetting theory. If there was enough evidence to show that Nick was an accomplice, "What else is there to talk about?" the judge asked, as if that were the end right then and there.

But in speaking, in having gotten caught up in the words and phrases and concepts that I had come to know so well, I had relaxed. My voice was steady. I was ready for this question and absolutely convinced we were in the right. The jury had not heard all of the evidence. If they had, they never would have found Nick guilty, even as an aider and abettor. I told the judges that the jury's guilty verdicts rested entirely on the theory that Nick did the shooting. I pointed out that even the lower federal court found that "the jury never deliberated on whether [Nick] was an aider and abettor." Given that the excluded evidence undermined the verdict reached, the state court was wrong in substituting its own judgment for the jury's.

I emphasized that the excluded witnesses would also have shown that Nick was not an accomplice. Pao and Tou would have told the jury that Nick got out of the car only after shots were fired, thinking he was being shot at by another gang. Pao and Tou would have told the jury that there was no discussion or agreement among them for Nick to follow the Prelude to the park. Pao and Tou would have explained to the jury why Nick had a gun that day, that it had been tossed into his lap by the actual shooter.

Most importantly, with a new trial, Nick would have told the jury that he had lied when he said, "It jammed." He hadn't wanted to shoot anyone. He hadn't tried to. He said the gun jammed because he was so afraid of what Pao Ma, the shooter and infamous gang leader, would have done to Nick or Nick's family if he couldn't explain why all the bullets were still in the chamber.

"This explanation is supported by the forensic evidence. The gun Nick had—the black weapon—did not malfunction," I concluded. "It did not jam. If that evidence had been given to the jury, it would have supported the evidence that Pao Ma acted alone. He surprised others in the car when he started shooting. He acted suddenly and without the support of my client."

I had made my most important point. I sat down.

The attorney general rose to make her presentation. I listened but disagreed with her points, writing furiously so I could rebut.

But then a judge interrupted:

*We really don't know what a jury would have done if the case
had been presented with the evidence. The jury was very concerned about who the shooter was. It took a long time to reach a
verdict. Juries do odd things. And sure, there was a fair amount of
evidence that would have suggested an aider and abettor, but we
just don't know. The jury might well have said, "He wasn't the
shooter" and returned a verdict of not guilty. We just don't know.*

The judge's words ended the argument. I actually felt hopeful.
At least one Ninth Circuit judge thought it was odd that the trial
court didn't let a jury hear all of the witnesses' testimonies just to
avoid a whole new trial.

The judges moved on to the next case, and I was left with a
glimmer of hope, a tiny ember. I had felt this before, of course, and
had been disappointed often enough that I should have known
better now. But I couldn't help it.

I motioned to Nick's family that we should leave the courtroom. Back in the hall, in almost a whisper, I told them, "We did
our best. Now all we can do is wait."

The long hallway was still quiet except for the steady sound
of my heels, each step amplified by the stone surrounding us. We
pushed through enormous glass doors, each covered by polished
brass bars, and into the bright sunlight and speeding traffic of San
Francisco. I shook hands with the mother, the sister, the friend.
The mother told her daughter to thank me. Then she repeated
her gratitude in her own language. I had the sense that she didn't
want to walk away, that she wanted to hug me or kiss my forehead or perform a rite I might not have seen before but that I
would understand in some fundamental way. I said a final goodbye
and—with a smile, through which I hoped to convey hope and
sympathy and sincerity—I turned and left.

We didn't wait long. About a month after the arguments in
court, the Ninth Circuit denied the appeal and upheld Nick's

convictions in a convoluted but scant one-and-a-half-page opinion. "The state court's conclusion that the plea structuring was not misconduct that 'infected the entire trial' was not objectively unreasonable."

The strange and subjective phrase "objectively unreasonable" was at the heart of this denial, as it is in the denial of thousands of habeas petitions every year. In this case, the prosecutor's plea bargains were wrong and unjust and inhumane, but the Ninth Circuit decided they did not rise to the level of "objectively unreasonable." I wanted to push back through those glass doors with their brass bars to find those three judges and scream that in this case, they were *wrong*.

Reading the paper a fourth time, I fixed on the Ninth Circuit's statement that even if the prosecutor *had* been wrong, "no other outcome of the trial would have been reasonably likely, particularly in light of aider and abettor liability under California law." Again, it simply did not matter that no jury had said that Nick was an aider and abettor. The judges of the Ninth Circuit deferred to the California judge who had heard the case ten years before. The California judge decided that Nick alone should bear the brunt of the punishment for the crimes.

I couldn't push through glass doors and scream at judges. I set the pages of the decision on my desk and—overwhelmed by the reality of it, and by the specter of the letter I would have to write to Nick that day—I let my head drop.

About a year after the United States Supreme Court denied reviewing his case and Nick Yang came to the very end of his legal challenges, he wrote to me.

Pao Ma had killed an innocent young man that day at the park. "But," Nick said, "in so many ways, he killed me too. I don't stop thinking about it—ever."

Nick's case brought a new sadness for me, a more intense kind of grief.

Between my hurried drive to Folsom State Prison on the first day to the afternoon when I sat at my desk reading the decision, the US Department of Justice subpoenaed my husband. I felt horrible for Nick, who was facing at least seventy-two years in prison for driving that car to the park. I felt awful for the victims of the shooting, kids playing basketball on a hot day in the Central Valley.

But the subpoena made my vision wider, deeper. The criminal justice system engulfed *many* more people than the convicted and the victims. I felt for Nick's stooped mother. I wished I had given her a hug that day on the busy San Francisco street corner. I felt for his sister and his beautiful friend, too young and hopeful to witness such organized inhumanity. I felt for Nick's father, who died, in part, of heartbreak. I felt for Pao Ma's mother, probably a lovely Hmong woman tending her garden in Merced just like my mother, but filled with sorrow for her son's violent and wasted life. I grieved for the children whose parents were in prison, parents who were absent for ten or twenty years at a time. I was sad that my father had missed my childhood. I was so sad for my husband and for our kids and our uncertain future.

The looming idea of prison hung over me and Doug in our dark bedroom on the afternoon we missed the event in San Francisco and for months after. I couldn't sleep. Instead of working, I found myself wandering paths in the Oakland hills, trying to focus on the smell of the bay trees. I couldn't plan Christmas, thinking the worst might happen by then. Logically, I knew the odds of anything serious coming of the subpoena were very slim. Still, logic would not cure fear. And the chronic fear I had developed after so many years in the criminal justice system had become contagious. Doug was sick with it.

I lay down beside my husband, accepted what he might or might not have done, and held on tightly.

CHAPTER 12

"ALL RISE!"

"**G**ood morning, Judge Forman," I said, making room on the bench seat of the hotel shuttle that would take us to court.

Judge Forman was the judge visiting from New York who had butchered me a year before at my oral argument in defense of Fetu Faraimo, my client from Guam. I was tickled by the coincidence of being in the same shuttle with a judge I remembered so well. I assumed his Honor had come back for more guest judging, preferring sunny Pasadena over the gray melting slush of a New York spring.

Judge Forman was not tickled. Although we won our case and the convictions were stricken from Faraimo's record and his resentencing was ordered, Judge Forman had written a scathing twenty-eight-page dissent. Twenty-eight pages of why I was wrong, why Faraimo was fairly punished, and why Betty Binns Fletcher was off her rocker. Her opinion, the published opinion of the court, was only ten pages.

The judge traveled with a duo of young and perky law clerks wearing clean, pressed suits, eager faces, and polished shoes. Each of them seemed to crane, following the judge as he turned slowly to see who dared to greet him from the back seat so cheerfully and at such at early hour.

"Good morning," he said. "How do I know you?"

"I'm Shanti Brien. I represented Fetu Faraimo in a case before you last year. Do you remember?"

I could almost smell the disdain wafting from him into the way, way back of the shuttle. His clerks laughed nervously with anticipation. They wondered what he would do to this pathetic lawyer, oblivious of the fury that my victory had ignited in the judge.

"I remember well." He faced forward purposefully.

After a few minutes of silence, he asked one of his clerks, "Did the US Attorney ask for rehearing?"

Both clerks shook their heads vigorously in unison. The losing party always has the option to ask the three-judge panel to reconsider the case or ask a nine-judge panel to consider it. Judge Forman's twenty-eight-page dissent invited the government to ask for rehearing, an invitation the government had so far declined.

Still delighting in my victory, lording it over them somewhat, I was disappointed that when we arrived at the courthouse, being in the back seat prevented the beautiful exit I had envisioned. I would not, as it turned out, be able to toss my hair and stride off into the courtroom, my defeated opponent left in my wake. Instead, they seemed to take extra time gathering their things. I found myself fumbling with the seat belt. As I stepped out—the judge right in front of me—my roller bag and briefcase tumbled onto the sidewalk.

"I just hope," the judge practically spat as I straightened up, "that you're here today for a more worthy client."

I stopped, shocked at his petty remark. Then I looked up at him.

"Yes, Your Honor."

I turned on my black high heel. Over my shoulder, just before disappearing into the courthouse, I called, "Have a great morning!"

| | | | |

Doug's fear made me want to help him more than ever before in our thirteen years of marriage or in the eighteen years I had been with him. And Doug wasn't acting tough. He wasn't the level-headed guy that misses a kick, loses the game, gets slaughtered by the newspapers, and still manages to stay focused on next week. He needed me. Not to keep our domestic world on track as he relentlessly organized and managed another remodel, not to listen to problems at work or frustrations with his mother. I didn't know how, exactly, but this subpoena was in my realm, and I would do something.

Basically, a subpoena amounts to a piece of paper that orders the recipient to come to court, attend a deposition, or produce documents. Courts don't issue subpoenas, attorneys do. But the court has the power to enforce a subpoena. Failing to respond means a person may be punished for contempt.

The only subpoena I ever issued was to a retired librarian from a California prison. My client claimed he couldn't get his habeas petition filed in time because the prison library was always closed. Every time he made a request, the librarian sent a note reading: "Due to illness of library staff, the library is closed." When my client produced the librarian's written excuses to the court, the judge thought my client had to have photocopied the same response over and over. A trial ensued, and I subpoenaed the librarian to testify. I spent several days with my head buried in the *Federal Rules of Civil Procedure*, researching the technical requirements of creating and serving the subpoena. Her objections could have been in the hundreds, but in the end, she just showed up. The force of a single piece of paper was amazing. A simple form printed out from the court's website summoned a woman with a gray bun atop her head, a gray cardigan sweater, and the directness only a prison employee could have. Her testimony, in the end, did not help my client as much as I would have liked, but her presence in court and her testimony were one of the many tiny victories my clients and I needed to hold onto. This victory was entirely due to a simple subpoena.

Doug's subpoena was not as simple. Government lawyers can issue subpoenas for investigatory purposes without any pending· litigation. The Anti-Trust Division of the Department of Justice issued the subpoena on Doug's company. Although technically this is an agency without the power to bring criminal charges, records gathered in response to agency subpoenas often lead to criminal charges. Incomplete responses may invite additional inquiry or even separate investigations for other federal crimes like obstruction of justice, obstruction of a federal proceeding, obstruction of a criminal investigation, witness tampering, or obstruction of a federal audit.

In the age of online communication, subpoenas for documents generally include emails sent and received. If you consider that the average business person sends and receives over one hundred emails per day,[14] and if a company has fifty employees and the subpoena requests all emails regarding a certain topic for five years, 1.25 million emails become relevant. They must be searched, coded, indexed and reviewed. They must be examined for content and for any privilege that would render them off-limits, such as attorney-client privilege or attorney work-product privilege. Privileged communications would be organized and listed on a privilege "log" but would not be sent to the government.

Real estate investors were being charged criminally for not complying with the subpoenas. The Justice Department sent out a press release with the headline blaring: "NORTHERN CALIFORNIA REAL ESTATE INVESTOR INDICTED ON AD-

---

14 Morgan, Jacob. "5 Ways Email Makes Your Employees Miserable." Forbes Magazine, 2013. https://www.forbes.com/sites/jacobmorgan/2013/10/15/5-ways-email-makes-your-employees-miserable/#14e9c53d1caa

DITIONAL CHARGE." A man from Danville, the small East Bay town where Doug grew up, had already been charged with conspiracy to commit bid rigging and fraud. He was now charged with obstruction of justice. After he "received a letter notifying him that a federal grand jury had subpoenaed his bank account," he allegedly "deleted and caused others to delete electronic records and documents related to the conspiracies." He also allegedly "installed and caused others to install and use a software program that overwrote deleted electronic records and documents so that they could not be viewed or recovered."[15] Desperation had caused Danville Man to dig himself even deeper.

The government also asked Doug's company to produce all documents related to all houses bought through an auction within the relevant time period. If you have ever bought a house, you know the truckloads of paperwork involved in buying or selling just one home. Doug bought over 100 homes using Lance as his bidding agent at the courthouse auctions. To reply to this subpoena would require superhuman organization, unrelenting patience, and the meticulousness of a lawyer.

Then, magic.

Somehow, Cris got out of her conflict. The superhuman, unrelenting, meticulous lawyer we had yearned for became *our* lawyer. I don't know how or why this happened. She fired a client? She helped the client settle his case and accept a plea bargain? We will never know, because she owes that client confidentiality. Technically, she represented Colin; practically, she joined our team. This is like Oprah joining your book club, or Martha Stewart joining your baking circle right before the county fair. Cris had the organization, the staunchness, the loyalty, and the connections. Once,

---

15 Press Release, Dept of Justice, May 8, 2013, http://www.justice.gov/atr/public/press_releases/2013/296523.htm

I had a client tell me they had been praying for an attorney for years, and then God delivered me. Now, I knew how that client felt.

Cris, with her polished blonde bob and raspy voice, had twenty or thirty years of experience representing corporate clients being investigated by the federal government. She was just enough older to feel authoritative, a trait reinforced by pantsuits that made her seem commanding and tough. But Cris saw beneath the polished corporate exterior and the defensive, resentful attitude of her clients. Happily for all of us, she thought Doug and Colin were just as cute as could be: sweet, hard-working and down-to-earth. She could see their good-heartedness, and she intended to defend it.

Cris and Mike, together with their law partners, associates, paralegals, assistants, and hired gatherers and copiers, worked for months to prepare a response to the subpoena. Doug's company's employees helped too.

Doug decided that the best medicine for him, his fail-safe cure for stress and anxiety, was work. Get-up-at-four-in-the-morning-and-work-non-stop-until-ten-at-night kind of work. He and Colin reasoned that by making the company bigger and better, expanding into different locations, hiring more employees, and investing in the infrastructure of the company, especially the technology, they would prove to all that they were legitimate. This was no shady, back-alley enterprise based on Lance's scams—not even close. The parallel and frenetic work of the lawyers and the company lasted for months.

Doug's company grew at an incredible rate. *San Francisco* magazine did a cover-story with full-color photos of Doug and Colin holding hammers in front of a home in Antioch, bright green sod only a couple of days old. T*he Wall Street Journal* regularly featured them on the front page of the business section. They were ranked the sixth fastest growing company in the Bay Area and named among the "Top 100 Most Innovative Entrepreneurs" by Goldman Sachs. They were widely considered to be the founders of a new industry—the large-scale ownership and management of single-family rental homes. There were large public companies that owned and managed apartment buildings, but no company had done the same with single-family homes. They were trailblazers.

Once Cris and Mike and Doug and Colin began to gather documents for the subpoena, no one seemed to need me. My focus turned to our family. Every night at dinner, each of us said what we were grateful for that day. Lilli often mentioned a cupcake or piece of chocolate someone gave her. Ceci was thankful for beating that one soccer team two years ago in the State Cup Tournament and fifty other things. She would go on and on until we cut her off to hear from the others. Two- then three-year-old Zach was consistently grateful for Big Trucks, then Teenage Mutant Ninja Turtles, then the Golden Ninja Lego guy.

What I didn't say to my kids was that I was thankful we had one of the best lawyers in the country on our side.

I was thankful that my marriage survived the NFL.

And as stressful and overwhelmed as I felt at times juggling three kids and twenty-some clients, I was thankful for my work.

As challenging as becoming a criminal defense lawyer had been, my practice had grown, and I had, too. I helped my clients, but they also helped me. I had been a quiet little girl who was afraid of men; I was now a competent, outspoken, professional woman. As a young woman, I had always said yes even when I meant no; now, I had a powerful voice I used to help others. Finally, I had an identity that felt right: I was a criminal defense attorney.

My clients were murderers and drug dealers and rapists, but many of them had been treated unfairly. They were the people our society despised, then forgot. It felt good to help them.

Of course, Christopher's harassing phone calls and sharp criticism felt like shit. And missing the Notice of Appeal deadline for the Mendozas still loomed unresolved as the judge considered my request for an extension. But the more time that passed from those cases, the less they stung. Pulling back and considering my career more widely, I felt solid. The intensity of the facts, the strength of legal posture, the trust and respect my clients showed me—all of that grounded me while also lifting me up. The weight of my professional life balanced the intensity of marriage and motherhood. I was an almost-forty-year-old woman, the mother of three, and a good wife. I was a good attorney, which gave me purpose and energy.

At times, I imagined myself on an episode of *LA Law*, arguing passionately for justice in a great-fitting suit before gray-haired judges who posed brilliant questions I answered with intelligence and grace. I imagined myself discovering the scrap of paper containing the shred of evidence lost or ignored by smart attorneys who had come before me. I would lift the paper in the courtroom, the audience turning in surprise and admiration as I won freedom for my misjudged and wrongly-convicted young client.

Of course, this was fantasy. My suit wasn't always perfectly pressed, the judges called me "Miss"—not "counselor," like they do on TV—and cases were won by hours of combing through briefs, never mysterious scraps of paper. But it didn't matter. I made my own money. I modeled powerful, professional womanhood for my three kids. I had important work to do all day: underscoring the unfairness of the "three-strikes" law; speaking out against racial discrimination in jury selection; developing the law barring juvenile shackling. I had long conversations with tearful mothers and girlfriends. I wrote good briefs in plain English. I asked for oral argument in every case. At a cocktail party, I could tell a great story about nearly every state prison in Northern California. Finally, I was becoming the lawyer I had always wanted to be.

Of course, my life as a lawyer had to fit into a larger (and sometimes surprising) framework. After the Vikings cut Doug mid-season, we had come back to the Bay Area, bought a house, and started to prepare for life after football. The minute we closed the deal on our Tudor-style home in the Oakland Hills, the New York Jets offered Doug a job. The girls and I didn't follow right away; I had a real job, and at ages five and three, the girls seemed a little more manageable, but we had to think about school. Our lives had become less nomadic.

By his second season, convinced that he wouldn't be coming home anytime soon, I felt I had a foundation on which I could support Doug and the tumult of a kicker's life. Being a criminal defense attorney, not just an NFL wife, actually gave me the freedom to be a better NFL wife. Because I could take my work with me, I decided we'd go to New York.

We rented a little furnished cottage on a beach in Long Island. The town had a pizza parlor, a small grocery store, and a fifteen-mile-per-hour speed limit. After dropping Lilli at pre-kindergarten in the church basement and Ceci at the babysitter's, I hurried back to my computer and the stack of papers in the corner of the bedroom. I prepared briefs and proofread them, I did online legal research and wrote letters to clients. I spent hours at Kinko's, copying and binding and mailing all of it back to California.

The New York winter, though, wore on the girls and me. Doug was working hard and not at the cottage a lot. Once Christmas was packed away, any magic that we had found in the snow and frost felt gone, too. Together, Doug and I decided the girls and I would return to California. The Jets had entered the playoff hunt, which meant Doug's last few games would be intense. We left in goodwill, the kids and I, partly because Doug had nailed the season. He wanted to finish strong to solidify his place for the next few years. Even he understood that he would be able to focus better with his wife and daughters settled back into life in the Bay Area. Over these two years with the Jets, he had made a remarkable 85 percent of his field goals, one of the best records in the league.

The Jets made the playoffs. In front of a rowdy group of family and friends who had travelled to San Diego, Doug made the game-winning field goal in the final minutes to secure the team's place in the AFC Championship. We erupted, screaming and dancing. And then we got really drunk.

Finally, it seemed that Doug's career had settled. After being cut by the Saints, being unemployed the next season, then cut by the Vikings, he had proven those teams wrong. I loved being at that game. I wasn't worried about crying babies, and I wasn't worried about what I was going to do with my life. I was too busy loving my husband and his day's victory.

Then, there was Pittsburgh.

The weekend after the San Diego game, the Jets were up against the Steelers, the victor moving on to the Super Bowl. In an icy, bitter wind, on a field that was mostly mud painted green so it would look like grass on TV, Doug missed two field goals within the last few minutes of the game. One of the kicks, from 47 yards, hit the left upright. A few inches to the right and the Jets would have won. I sat in our little living room in Oakland, Ceci on my lap, and stared at the TV in disbelief. On the heels of his best season ever, one of the best seasons for any kicker in NFL history, my husband had had the worst game of his career.

The *New York Press* called it "the biggest kick he will ever attempt and he missed it. Twice." Another paper said, "Kicking in Heinz Field is tough. It's hell. And hell welcomed Doug Brien." There on the couch, the girls and I descended into our own hell of helpless watching.

The next morning, the *New York Daily News* reported that "like countless Jets fans across the country, Shanti Brien was heartbroken Saturday night."

"I feel for him," I had told the reporter, even though I hated him for calling me at home and I hated him for what he would write about my husband. I was quoted as saying: "Honestly, I hope the New York media shows some mercy, or it could make a bad situation worse, to be truthful. Everyone makes mistakes. I hope people can understand that."

The article ended by saying that his kids would be so happy to have Doug home. And Doug *was* relieved to be home now that the season was over, away from the reporters and the frigid New York winter. He thought I shouldn't have talked to the reporter, but I think he loved that I defended him. The end was near, the NFL chapter of our story was essentially over.

| | | | |

The story of Fetu Faraimo, the Samoan man from Guam who allowed me victory over Judge Forman, would not end. When I returned from Pasadena and my hotel-shuttle meeting with his Honor, I received notice that the Ninth Circuit requested briefs from the US Attorney and me on whether Mr. Faraimo's case should be heard *en banc*. Nine judges of the Ninth Circuit could review the decision made by the three judges, then reverse or affirm the decision.

Forman had asked for this review. Although the rules allow a judge to ask for a vote on whether the case should be reconsidered by a larger panel, in practice, I had never heard of the court doing this without one side requesting it.

Apparently, seeing me had reminded him of what he saw as the waste of judicial resources going to criminals in prisons who were writing habeas petition after habeas petition. If I had kept quiet, just savored my victory and enjoyed the ride in the mini-van pretending I had no idea who the judge was, I was convinced my client's victory would not be at risk. Judge Forman seemed intent on slamming the brakes on that runaway habeas train, and now it felt like he was out to stop me too.

Immediately, I began to get inquiries from the Supreme Lurkers, as I dubbed them. Lurkers are lawyers in Washington, D.C.

who want to argue in front of the Supreme Court. They regularly follow decisions that come out of the Ninth Circuit with strong dissents. Those are decisions that are ripe for Supreme Court review. Any decision made by Betty Binns Fletcher would be all the better, because the US Supreme Court loves nothing more than overturning the West Coast liberal block that masquerades as the Ninth Circuit Court of Appeal.

I hadn't known anything about the Lurkers until this arrived in my inbox:

Ms. Shanti—

Congratulations on the victory in the Ninth Circuit in Mr. Faraimo's case. I have been following his appeals for years, and I was amazed that the Ninth Circuit came out the way that it did. I am writing to offer whatever assistance I can to Mr. Faraimo in opposing the Government's inevitable petition for certiorari, as Mr. Faraimo's case is the sort that our firm would probably agree to take pro bono.

By way of background, I am a general litigator who tries to keep an active pro bono practice. I am not one of the old hands of the Supreme Court bar, and you will doubtlessly start hearing from them. But I have a decent idea about what persuades the Justices—I clerked for [a Supreme Court Justice] in 2002—and I can promise a client like Mr. Faraimo a real commitment of time and attention.

One personal note: it is my understanding that Mr. Faraimo is Samoan. I speak and understand Samoan, and he and I probably have friends and relatives in common. It would be a real honor and privilege to have the opportunity to represent a Samoan before the Supreme Court.

In all events, please do not hesitate to contact me if I can provide further information or answer questions. Look forward to hearing from you.

Warmest regards,

[Mr. Supreme Lurker]

I was at once honored, confused, and scared shitless. He was watching Mr. Faraimo's case? I had no idea anyone watched the case, read the opinion, or cared at all. The "old hands of the Supreme Court bar?" Should I be booking my ticket to D.C. to defend the results of my hard-won case? The decision would be in peril. Mr. Faraimo's convictions could be upheld and my greatest legal victory redacted. If the case was headed to the Supreme Court, I didn't intend to deliver it, gift wrapped, to some Lurker. This was my case. A lawyer's career can be made legendary by arguing well before the Supreme Court. The thought of it overwhelmed me with nervousness and self-doubt, but I had earned any chance the case presented. Judge Betty Binns Fletcher, the Lioness of Liberalism, had written a great opinion, and I would defend it.

I have never worked harder than I did on the brief addressing whether the case should be heard *en banc*. I spent hundreds of hours reading Judge Forman's dissent, reading the cases he cited, dissecting his arguments and crafting a response. I hired a former Ninth Circuit clerk to read it over to offer feedback and edits.

In the end, the government said they didn't want the decision reviewed either. I should have known, because they hadn't asked for review when they had their chance. It appeared no one wanted review except Judge Forman and a handful of Lurkers.

I don't know what judicial bargaining went on behind the scenes, but when the court issued the opinion denying *en banc* review, they also issued an amended decision on Mr. Faraimo's case. And it was worse than a Supreme Court review. In this new decision, they had changed a few crucial words. Several references to "manifest injustice" were removed, along with the most significant sentence, in my opinion, of the decision.

The sentence used to read: "We reverse and remand to the district court with instructions to issue the writ of habeas corpus, vacate Faraimo's convictions for importation, and resentence Faraimo on the remaining counts." The concluding sentence of the new opinion simply read, "We REVERSE and REMAND to the district court with instructions to issue the writ of habeas corpus and vacate Faraimo's convictions for importation."

The judges were no longer ordering resentencing. Faraimo could "win" and have his convictions stricken from his record, but he could not go in front of a judge to ask for a new sentence on his remaining convictions. Even after three of his six convictions were lifted, he would still owe four life sentences plus a thirty-year sentence, all to run concurrently.

Judge Forman may have lost the war against endless habeas petitioners, but he had definitely won his battle against Faraimo. Our victory meant virtually nothing without resentencing. It might have been a moral victory for Faraimo, but he was a man who wanted to see his five kids someday; now, he would not, in fact, make it home to Guam to hug them.

Again, I persevered. I called, wrote, and emailed the public defender in Guam, with increasing concern and bitterness when he ignored my communications. Faraimo needed a public defender to represent him in federal court. I was not qualified to practice in Guam, and I did not have expertise in the federal sentencing guidelines—a maze of rules and charts that federal public defenders used every day.

Yet, after a year of trying and not finding anyone more qualified, I wrote the Motion for Resentencing and Request for Ap-

pointment of Counsel, and Faraimo filed it himself. He had a decent argument: without the three importation counts, the amount
of methamphetamine could not reach the 1000-gram threshold
to justify a mandatory life sentence.

A year after Faraimo filed the motion, the court finally appointed the Federal Public Defender of Guam to represent him.
The year following that, the public defender filed a motion. A
third year passed before the Guam District Court said they did
not have jurisdiction to resentence Faraimo. The judges did not
know which court did, but it wasn't Guam. Faraimo's case was a
hot potato no one wanted to get caught holding.

Then, months later, on a Wednesday afternoon that felt like
any other Wednesday, I got a call from a young lawyer in Los
Angeles. He sounded barely old enough to have a driver's license.
He spoke with a youthful eagerness that reminded me of myself
when I was starting out in appeals. He was chatty and resourceful
and looking for some insider wisdom on his new case. The court
had appointed him to represent Fetu Faraimo.

Early in the conversation, I asked how he, specifically, was the
one appointed, given that many in the federal public defender
office could have gotten the case.

"I'm Jewish" he said, as if the connection were obvious.

I asked him to repeat himself.

"The case came into the Federal Public Defender on Christmas Eve. I'm about the only one who works that day."

"Well, Merry Christmas, huh?" I said with a laugh. It felt like
a gift to have some young energy helping my old client.

"I know! I'm excited," he said.

He explained that he happened to be discussing Faraimo's
case with his supervising attorney. She responded by telling him
to look up a case from years back, a great victory out of the Ninth
Circuit; it had something to do with convictions for importation

being struck down. That great victory was mine! And, incredibly, Faraimo's—the very case this young man had been assigned!

The call reminded me what an amazing case it was: after so many years of battling the legal system on his own, I had helped Faraimo—a poor, uneducated Samoan father-of-five—to be heard by some of the most important judges in the world, judges who then agreed with his arguments. Our failed attempts at getting Faraimo a new, reduced sentence had discouraged me, but I was enlivened by this kid, this Jesse Gessin—energetic and enterprising—who was freshly on the case.

By the time I hung up, after forty-five minutes of listening to this young attorney, I thought we might finally win resentencing for Mr. Faraimo. This lawyer dealt with the complex federal sentence guidelines every day, he was eager, and he had the energy to see it through. He was the perfect attorney for us to hand the case over to.

The timing was also perfect. In the recent past, the War on Drugs had incarcerated poor people of color like Mr. Faraimo at staggering rates. Sentences for drugs crimes, especially harsh mandatory minimum sentences that give judges no leeway to craft sentences commensurate with the culpability of the defendants, typically exceed sentences for rape, murder, and arson. These sentences had filled our prisons beyond capacity.

But change was underway. The disparity between sentences related to crack cocaine and powered cocaine had already been reduced. At one time, possession of one ounce of crack earned the same as 100 ounces of powered cocaine. Because crack cocaine had been more popular in black neighborhoods, the 100-1 sentencing disparity translated to disproportionately harsh sentences for black defendants. In the later years of his service, former Attorney General Eric Holder, of the Obama administration, spoke often for changes in the mandatory minimum sentences for drug offenses.

In this context, young Jesse began working diligently for Faraimo. In his first conversation with the Assistant US Attorney, the same woman I had argued against in the Ninth Circuit, she mentioned this would be an easy case because the district court did not have jurisdiction to resentence Faraimo, and even if the district court had jurisdiction, he was serving a mandatory minimum life sentence. Jesse and I understood, though, that the case was anything but easy.

First, Jesse faced a jurisdictional problem. The federal court in LA basically asked Jesse to prove it was the right court. There was also the fact that the Ninth Circuit panel struck the word "resentencing" from the original remand order. How could he argue for resentencing when the court had specifically not ordered it? Jesse's answer was the writ of *audita querela defendentis*—not a spell from Harry Potter, but an 800-year-old writ that was last issued in federal court in the 1980s.

Yet, like magic, two important events coincided: research attorneys working at the federal district court decided that the court *did have* jurisdiction to resentence, and California passed Proposition 47, which allowed defendants serving three-strikes sentences for minor offenses to get their sentences reduced.

To prepare for resentencing, Jesse set out to "reclassify" Faraimo's prior felonies as misdemeanors, and thus rid his record of strikes. Without those two "strikes," Faraimo wouldn't be eligible for a mandatory minimum life sentence.

"At one point at the court in Long Beach," Jesse told me over the phone, "I was directed from Department 1 to Department 18 to Department 24 back to Department 1. These were, after all, thirty-year-old felonies!"

But after months of leg-work and telephone jockeying, Jesse got Faraimo's felonies reduced to misdemeanors. Jesse then sent a letter to the government—350 pages, including exhibits—asking for them to agree to a sentence at the low-end of the sentencing guidelines and without a mandatory minimum. The exhibits included all of Faraimo's accomplishments in prison: he mentored at-risk Pacific-Islander inmates; he had hundreds, if not thousands of hours of education, sometimes taking the same class multiple times; he had not had a serious infraction in over a decade.

So, on a warm day in Oakland, as I sat at my desk giving last thoughts as to what I would present in the Law and Public Policy class I was teaching at Mills College, I got a call from an unknown Los Angeles number. Usually I would let it go to my voicemail, but something made me pick up.

"Hey!" the caller said. "This is Jesse."

We hadn't spoken for six months or more.

"Fetu Faraimo got resentenced yesterday. Two-hundred forty months."

My hand started to shake. I didn't say anything.

"Shanti, are you there? That's time served! He's going home to Guam! I should have called you yesterday. I knew you wanted to know. Things just got so crazy and—"

"I wish I could have been there. This is ... amazing! Amazing."

In 1997, at the height President Bush's War on Drugs, Fetu Faraimo had received four life sentences plus thirty years, a mind-bogglingly long term, due to mandatory minimum sentences. Ironically, because Faraimo's legal journey took nearly twenty years, during half of which I accompanied him, he caught up with the slow reformation of what has been a racist, illogical, unjust War on Drugs.

Recently, the federal First Step Act of 2018 made significant (while still insufficient) changes in this area. It made retroactive the 2010 law which reduced the crack cocaine and powder cocaine sentencing disparity. This will affect nearly 2,600 federal inmates, according to the Marshall Project. The First Step Act also began to address the mandatory minimum sentencing disaster, expanding the "safety valve" that judges can use to avoid the harsh sentences, reducing the automatic sentence for three or more convictions from life to twenty-five years, and restricting the "stacking" of gun charges against drug offenders.

Even after passage of "the most significant criminal justice reform legislation in years," the federal system remains acutely focused on drug crimes. In 2019, there are still almost half a million people incarcerated for non-violent drug offenses in this country,[16] accounting for one in five of all incarcerated people. In federal prisons, almost half of the entire population is there for a drug crime.[17]

Several politicians have proposed taking the reforms to the next step. Using the Executive Branch's clemency power for people in federal prison, policy makers could release those imprisoned for marijuana-related offenses, those who would have benefited from the First Step Act if it had been applied retroactively, and those still incarcerated under the crack cocaine sentencing penalties that, despite numerous attempts, still remain harsher than those for powder cocaine. It's estimated this could impact an additional 17,000-20,000 people.

Of course, almost *100 times* that number of people are incarcerated based on state court convictions. With over a million arrests for drug possession alone in the US every year—many of those leading to convictions—the War on Drugs is still raging.

But even if we could get all low-level drug offenders and other War on Drug casualties out of prison, we'd be left with three major problems. First, we give out years in prison to people like I dole out Tums to my kids. ("Yes, two might do the job, but why not take 15?!?") Fetu Faraimo is a good example. What does four

---

16 Sawyer, Wendy and Peter Wagner. "Mass Incarceration: The Whole Pie 2019." The Prison Policy Initiative, March, 2019. https://www.prisonpolicy.org/reports/pie2019.html.

17 75,957 people or 45.3% as of June 15, 2019: https://www.bop.gov/about/statistics/statistics_inmate_offenses.jsp

life sentences plus thirty years even mean? Nick got a sentence of 77 years. The massive amount of waste, in both human potential and actual resources, is hard to comprehend. According to the Legislative Analyst's Office, a non-partisan fiscal advisory to the California legislature, it costs taxpayers $81,000 per year to keep someone in prison. That is over $6.2 million for my client Nick alone without even accounting for the opportunity cost of his wasted life and the damage to the health and wellbeing of his entire family and community. With the economic, social, and health care challenges facing us in the next fifty years, we just *have* to find a better way to prevent and respond to crime.

Secondly, we must face the collateral damage of millions of people, mostly people of color, with criminal convictions. Putting aside the psychological and physical toll of living in prison, formerly incarcerated people face obstacles at every turn. Getting jobs, securing housing, getting government assistance, going on fieldtrips with their kids who attend public schools—all of these may be impossible with felony convictions and sometimes less. Of course, most felons lose the right to vote, which is essential to making reforms to the broken system that profoundly impacts them. Over six million people cannot vote because of a conviction; to put that in perspective, Hillary Clinton won the popular vote by 2.87 million votes in 2016. But those convicted of crimes lose seemingly more mundane opportunities to participate and thrive in civic life, too, like getting many professional licenses and having a beer with friends. Probation and parole conditions micro-manage the lives of over seven million Americans, often leading to re-incarceration. The hyper-control of those who have already "paid" society for their crimes prevents them from re-integrating into life on the "outside" and finding alternatives to re-offending, and ultimately, prevents all of us from re-building safe, thriving communities.

I can't help but think of Deandra Jones. She lived as a hard-working bookkeeper and single mother before being sent to prison for seven years. She has most likely completed her sentence and returned to Sacramento. I imagine she may have spent months or years looking for work (it being nearly impossible to find a professional position as a convicted felon). Without the high-paying job she once had, Deandra may need government assistance for housing and food, but those are unavailable to her. Getting custody of her two daughters would be challenging as well. So, even if we assume she was, at worst, a get-away driver, and at least, a young African American who "talked ghetto," she received an incredibly harsh sentence: seven years in prison, a life of under-employment and instability, and irreparable damage to her family.

Finally, the remaining criminal justice system, even if it gets smaller, will not necessarily be fairer. In *The New Jim Crow*, Professor Michelle Alexander argues (quite convincingly, I believe) that the criminal justice system is a system of racial oppression. The racially disparate outcomes, in terms of convictions and sentences, are not caused by individual racist police, prosecutors, and judges (although, of course, they contribute to the problems), but are rather the intended outcome of the system, not unlike the outcomes of the previous system of racial oppression, Jim Crow. Subscribing to this theory makes it awfully hard to "improve" the criminal justice system or make it more "fair." We would have to completely dismantle criminal justice as we know it.

I just can't get behind this. I am an attorney, after all, and not an activist. I am an incrementalist by training and afraid of change by personality. I also recognize the privilege and power I get from my work within the system, which of course, I would lose if it were dismantled. Finally, although I was frustrated by the rate of change of the typical ligation model of representing one client at a time, I have increasingly witnessed substantial progress due to anti-bias education and empathy building.

Besides the structural inequities built into the criminal justice system—like the crack/powder cocaine disparity—the implicit racial biases of participants at each stage of the system reinforces and perpetuates those inequities. For example, a police officer might glance past the young white kid on the corner and more quickly arrest the young African American man with him. The prosecutor would offer the African American man six years in prison instead of four, and despite the public defender's urging to him to take the deal ("because he probably did it anyway"), the African American defendant would go to trial. There, the mostly-white jury might interpret the nervous behavior on the street corner as evidence of guilt rather than fear of the police and would find the young man guilty. The judge might feel that this young man is not going to turn it around and sentence our African American man to eight years in prison. If he had been arrested, the young white kid might have gotten six months' probation. All of this could happen without a racist in the bunch.

I am convinced that raising awareness of implicit biases, their pervasiveness and profound impact on outcomes, and teaching criminal justice professionals the tools and strategies to reduce those biases, can create a system that is fairer and more just. It's an incremental approach, not unlike the challenge to Fetu Faraimo's convictions for importation. At first that seemed like a small step, but it ended up leading to a huge victory.

I believe that Fetu Faraimo, Jesse Gessin, and I won a small battle in a very large fight for justice.

The fight must go on.

CHAPTER 13

ACCEPTANCE OF RESPONSIBILITY

O n a spring day in 2012, Lance Jones entered the formal federal courtroom. Wood paneling, upholstered seats that fold down like those in a theatre, and low-pile carpeting kept the mood somber. No one spoke above a whisper. As opposed to the chaos of county courtrooms—the backbone of the state system, where public defenders attempt to reduce bail for a client in an orange jumpsuit and whole shackled lines of defendants shuffle in and wait hours in the jury box, joking and rattling their cuffs—the federal courtroom is quiet. A few well-dressed attorneys sit in dark suits, their clients silent at their sides.

The judge called Lance's case. She called forth his attorney. She probably straightened her robe and adjusted the small microphone as she said, "Is your client prepared to enter a plea?"

"He is, Your Honor."

When Doug was served with the subpoena by the US Department of Justice in early 2011, a national widespread attack on mortgage fraud was just heating up. Between 2010 and 2013, the Department of Justice filed nearly 10,000 financial fraud cases against nearly 15,000 defendants, including more than 2,900 mortgage fraud defendants. On Christmas Eve, 2014, the Department announced that in the Northern California district, mortgage fraud cases had yielded fifty-one plea agreements and five indictments. Of almost 3,000 mortgage fraud cases throughout the country, Northern California would get, at most, fifty-six convictions. And Lance was one.

He pled guilty as part of a plea agreement that his attorney and government lawyers had been crafting for months. The plea proceeding transcripts are only a brief segment of the formal agreement that was typed, reviewed, edited, and endlessly re-negotiated.

The judge carefully informed Lance of all of the rights he would give up by pleading guilty. In so many cases, the words seem shallow, the whole process a formality. But thinking of Jake Mendoza's guilty plea, the plea scheme in Nick Yang's case, and the plea bargains that prosecutors squeeze out of over-charged and desperate people, I imagined the weight of each of these fundamental rights. The judge said Lance gave up the right to trial by jury; the right to be presumed not guilty; the right to confront and cross-examine witnesses against him. He gave up the right to subpoena witnesses on his behalf; the right to remain silent; the right to appeal his conviction. He gave up the right to appeal the imposition of the sentence on him.

Lance pled guilty to two counts: conspiracy to suppress and restrain competition through bid rigging, and conspiracy to commit mail fraud. He admitted that he committed those crimes and that he earned no less than $524,039 by committing them. He agreed that the maximum possible sentence he could receive was forty years in prison and a fine of $2 million.

But Lance would not be put away for forty years, and he knew it. The whole point of the bargain was to avoid the maximum sentence. Instead, the parties balanced the aggravating and mitigating factors set by Federal Sentencing Guidelines. In aggravation, Lance caused a monetary loss over $400,000 and had more than ten victims. He also played an "aggravating role" in the conspiracy. Still, because he pled guilty, Lance's sentence would be reduced significantly, as he showed "acceptance of responsibility." Ultimately, Lance would be sentenced to a prison term between three-and-a-half and four-and-a-half years. He would pay a fine between $7,500 and $75,000, in addition to repaying the $524,039.

This sentence is essentially established in advance by the Federal Sentencing Guidelines. These guidelines create a formula based on criminal history, the type of crime, and the "points" added and reduced by the aggravating and mitigating factors. Still, the judge imposes the sentence she deems fair and appropriate. She can sentence him to the agreed-upon number of years or not. A probation officer will learn salient details of Lance's life and share them with the court: his childhood, education, family, his debts and his bank account balances, criminal history and traffic infractions. I once represented a mother of three children who received prison instead of probation partly based on her "extensive history of disobeying authority," supposedly evidenced by a series of speeding tickets in the years before her conviction. She went to prison because of speeding tickets!

Lance's sentence also depended greatly on whether Lance, in the time between entering a plea and receiving his sentence, provided "substantial assistance in a Federal Proceeding." There are many reasons why a judge may grant a "downward departure" (less time in prison than the guideline sentence) or an "upward departure." One important way that a defendant can earn a downward departure is to "provide substantial assistance in the investigation or prosecution of another person who has committed an offense."[18]

---

18 United States Sentencing Guidelines section 5K1.1.

This means he helps the government convict someone else. Like Pao Ma helped the prosecutor convict Nick Yang of the shooting Pao Ma himself did, Lance would detail everything he knew about everyone involved in the bid-rigging conspiracy or any other related crimes. He would provide written affidavits and ultimately testify at the trials of those who refuse to take a plea. He would provide the government evidence, and the government would ask the judge to reduce the sentence.

Yet, he would only receive this opportunity if the United States Attorney deemed him worthy. Lance's plea agreement stated explicitly that the "United States may request, and the defendant will not oppose, that sentencing be postponed until his cooperation is complete." This is not unlike Nick Yang and his co-defendants, the Hmong gang members each scrambling to take pleas before the others. The government doesn't allow the defendant who pled guilty to actually receive the benefit of the plea agreement until that defendant has done what the government demands. For Nick's co-defendants, that meant staying quiet and not admitting that Pao Ma was the real shooter until Nick had been convicted. For Lance, this meant he would not be sentenced until the trials of the hold-out members of the conspiracy were completed. This would take years.

So, Lance—the man who had bought over 100 homes for Doug's fledgling company—was out on bail, and most likely desperate to provide every morsel of evidence to the government that held his freedom in its immense hand of discretion.

| | | | |

The judge deciding the fate of Jake Mendoza, whose freedom had been imperiled by the deadline I had forgotten, granted us leniency. Jake would be allowed to appeal the denial of his habeas petition based on his claim that his lawyer did not adequately explain the plea bargain to him. He could appeal, even though I had missed the deadline.

The court had, apparently, seen that the struggles of raising three small children were significant enough to confuse whether a deadline was thirty or sixty days from a certain Tuesday in May. While the impact for Jake was potentially far larger, I was also keenly aware that a less sympathetic decision by the judge also might have undermined my entire career. By either public discipline by the State Bar or just word-of-mouth through the small appellate community, my professional reputation would have been damaged.

I received the call just hours before Doug's fortieth birthday party. Friends poured into our house, bringing bottles of Scotch and whiskey and fan gear emblazoned with the Cal Bear for the birthday boy. During the party, Doug pulled me aside. He thanked me for all the effort that had gone into the party. But then my generous, outward-thinking husband took the time during his fortieth celebration, to say, "It sounds like you and your client received the real gifts." He gave me a big, whiskey-smelling hug, and I believed him.

I had been given the gift of mercy. In the endless hours I spent thinking about the judge's decision, I devised three possibilities to explain his generosity: he had been the victim of harassment from an overbearing, threatening client; he was just plain shocked by the outlandish confluence of flat warts, OCD, pinworms, toddlerhood, and lice; or, he believed it was simply not right to punish Jake for my mistake. Whatever the reason, his decision seemed like forgiveness, and the relief was physical.

But it appeared, as always, that *my* mistake would be easily forgiven, where my client's would not. A few months later, the Ninth Circuit denied our request for an appeal. I tried to remind myself that the system survived on convictions and depended on preserving them at all costs. I could not change that.

At least Jake had his father to provide him forgiveness. Or maybe not quite forgiveness, but an understanding that everyone makes mistakes—some worse than others, but human mistakes nonetheless. Jake would be supported by his father, his mother, and his four brothers. They would visit him in prison. They would bring magazines and ten family photos to each visit—the limit—no larger than the maximum size, 8x10. They would tell him all about their aunt and her small wedding on the coast near Mendocino. They would hold Jake tight at the beginning of the visit, hug him until the guards asked them to step back, and when they sat at the linoleum tables, they would share all the stories they could until their family time together was up.

| | | | |

Just as my children settled into homework at the farm table and I set another plate in the dishwasher, my father pushed through the kitchen door. A leather bag was slung over his shoulder, and he carried a paper sack from the dollar store in one hand and a flute made of PVC pipe in the other.

"I'm here," he announced, "and I've brought Rubik's Cubes. One for you, one for Doug, one for Lilli, one for Ceci, and a double-sided one here for Zach. We could all learn how to solve it together, then write down the algorithms!"

I couldn't quite call him Dad or Paw-paw. I just didn't know him that well.

"Hey, Hal!" I said.

He had arrived to watch the kids while Doug and I went to dinner. He lives about a mile away in a facility for people over fifty-five that has some affordable units. My father—the mathematical genius, sketcher of gorgeous life-like bears, the man who thought his daughter might like to see him, for the first time in years, in full clown-face—is on Social Security disability now. He cannot hold a job, at sixty-three-years-old, because he suffers from chronic severe depression. Because I am his closest relative, he asked me to be his representative payee. I receive his Social Security checks, and I pay his two bills: rent and electricity. Just as he might have done for me thirty-five years ago, in a wholly different kind of childhood, I was the one to give him an allowance each week.

"Thanks, Hal," I said. And I meant it. "I really appreciate you coming."

He has apologized so many times for leaving me and my mom. His depression, unrecognized and untreated, controlled him. He never used this as an excuse, exactly. But understanding his difficulties has helped me to understand the reality of my childhood. He has made amends by jumping into the role of grandfather, by planting a tidy vegetable garden for us last spring and by fixing the hooks in the bathroom when they came loose earlier this fall.

"This is paradise up here," he said, mostly to me, but looking out the window, then at my three kids. "This house. These beautiful children reading and doing math."

Strangely, it was during those years of investigation—while Doug and I waited to hear what would happen after we supplied the government with everything they needed—that I really experienced the "paradise" that my father saw. Doug and I had survived the NFL, with its 80 percent divorce rate for retired players. Lilli outgrew her strange illnesses and found a passion for volleyball. Ceci deep-breathed her way out of the crying fits. Little Zach thrived as a toddler, but even as he grew, he loved kisses all over his face and neck, and I never tired of pulling him close. Doug's vulnerability and humility wore away built-up resentment.

Still, we had been waiting years to hear if anything would happen with the federal investigation. The Feds can be likened to sleeping dogs, and we planned to let them lay. But the waiting was unbearable. The not-knowing felt endless, as months of no news turned into years. With time, like any trauma, the acute pain faded and slowly, slowly we got used to living with it. But it was like sleeping in a sandy bed, a constant low-grade concern we could never truly forget.

We distracted ourselves with work. The daily routine of packing lunches and driving the carpool, fixing the clogged toilet and sifting through emails—all of that absorbed most of our time. We found hours to hike together as a family in the dry hills of the East Bay; when I breathed in the smell of bay leaves, I could only hope that we would continue to have the luxury of Doug at home with us on the weekends, during the week, for holidays and celebrations. Together on those hikes, Doug and I would stand looking over caramel-colored hills layered all the way to Mt. Diablo where he grew up. We listened to the kids running and laughing on the dirt trail. In some ways, it was hard to believe we had made it that far.

Then, one day late in the spring almost four years after he had received the subpoena, Doug was striding toward the elevator through the marble and glass space of his firm's lobby, when he was stalled by a familiar face. There, on the leather bench, slightly hunched and dwarfed by the soaring windows, Lance Jones sat in reception, in his fancy low-slung jeans. Only after Doug had passed did he recognize Lance.

He kept walking. He slid into the elevator.

Not until a few hours later did Lance text. "I was trying to see you earlier. Can you talk?"

Doug had been counseled to have no contact whatsoever with Lance. He had been specifically advised against this.

"I'm in the area all afternoon," Lance wrote. "Let me know."

He texted a few more times that afternoon. He pushed the idea of talking. Even for a few minutes. He explained that he had a new business partner; he wanted Doug to meet him.

Doug said he felt doubt before worry washed over him. He couldn't be at all sure what Lance might do. He had made subtle threats over the years that "something" might happen to the houses he had purchased for Doug's company. Lance had purchased the titles to the houses on the courthouse steps, so he knew all of the addresses. Doug feared vandalism. He worried about trumped-up lawsuits and, of course, he was scared of what Lance might say to the government if Doug didn't appease him with a short meeting.

Doug tucked in his shirt and went down to the lobby. He hadn't seen Lance in years—hadn't been in the same room with him or spoken to him—yet for hour upon hour, hundreds of hours, Doug had forced his brain to remember every detail of every conversation between them. He had spent days replaying every phone call with Lance to lawyers and analyzing every word of every email. He spent weeks of his life worrying about how this man could have misinterpreted one word here, one phrase there, anything to indicate that Doug wanted to be part of the conspiracy. During the past four years, my husband had been forced to think almost obsessively about the man he now agreed to speak with briefly, the man now standing in his lobby with slicked-back hair and an outstretched hand.

"Is there a place we could talk?" Lance looked around. The lobby opened up to views of Lake Merritt, young Oaklanders jogging by.

"I'm not wired. I just want you to know," Lance said.

"Yeah," Doug said. "Okay."

"So, turns out I'm taking the fall for everyone. I've got this massive fine. Like a million dollars," Lance launched in, spewing details before they could move anywhere private. "I'm going to jail, man."

Doug just looked at him, hands in his pockets.

"I'm in a bad way. I need to make some money. My business partner's here. I need this, man. To pay the fine."

Doug felt very weird, but thought, *Fine, I'll meet the guy for a minute.*

They walked to the corner café. An older man, starting to gray, sat alone at a corner table. His phone was face down in front of him. He didn't get up when Doug and Lance came in. He shook Doug's hand but averted his eyes. He looked to Lance.

"Hey, flip that phone over," Lance said. "I don't want Doug thinking we're recording him."

Doug was certain at that point that he was being recorded. He planned only to listen to Lance, to say little, and to leave as soon as possible.

Instead of talking about their new business, Lance kept talking about the fine. How big it was, how impossible to pay off, how desperate he was.

"If you can just get me the money to start this up, this business, Doug, I'll take care of you," Lance offered. "I want you to know I never said anything about you guys. I like you guys."

The supposed business partner stared at Lance but seemed to have no idea about any work they would ever do together. He concentrated on every word, barely glancing at Doug.

Doug had no idea what Lance meant by "taking care of him." It wasn't clear if this was an attempt at extortion, a trap set up by the government to get Doug to admit to something illegal, or if it was actually a desperate plea on the part of a desperate man. Regardless of motive, the twice-mentioned audio recording, the poor acting skills of the "partner," and the complete lack of details about the supposed business led Doug to believe that the feds were not involved. The whole scene seemed like a B-rated movie about a botched sting operation; Doug liked to think the US government would do a better job.

Extortion remained a possibility, Doug paying Lance to guarantee that he would say nothing to the government. Lance easily could have threatened to tell the Department of Justice that Doug had explicitly agreed to Lance's plan to pay others to stop bidding on the houses that Doug wanted. In exchange for silence, Doug would have to pay.

Doug said, "I can't help you, Lance." He spoke clearly, flatly. He could not help with the new business, and he would not be extorted.

"Come on, man. You don't understand. I just need some money. No work? You don't have anything for me?"

Doug knew then that it was desperation.

"Let me explain this to you very clearly," my husband said. "I run a public company. I can't be involved in this. I need to go."

As Doug rose to leave, Lance and the other man seemed surprised. Speechless, they watched Doug walk quickly back toward the building. He returned to the lobby with the soaring windows that framed the stretch of blue sky. A horizontal sliver of the lake shined beyond the building. Doug rode the elevator to the twenty-third floor and collapsed into his chair.

After dinner that night, when Zach was tucked in and we had the newspaper scattered over our bed, I listened to my husband tell me all about the visit from the man who was the reason for our four years of panic and worry. I was surprised that Doug had waited the whole day to tell me, but so thankful to be safe in our big bed, under a thick white comforter, with our kids safely in the house and the doors locked. I was scared of Lance and his increasing desperation, even if I didn't actually know about the violence in his future.

CHAPTER 14

THE WHOLE TRUTH
AND NOTHING
BUT THE TRUTH

I believed that David Tuggle—accused rapist, possessor of one dose of methamphetamine, three-striker, and one very respect-ful older gentleman—was innocent.

I had first contacted the Northern California Innocence Proj-ect only a week or so after meeting with Tuggle in the cramped space at Folsom State Prison in 2007. I believed he had been accused falsely by Debra. She had given him her phone number. She casually entered the convenience store to buy a lemonade and chewing gum with him. The attorney at the Innocence Project seemed interested right away, especially as I explained how the police at the line-up had told the second alleged victim, "No, not that one. Don't you think it might be this one? We've arrested him for another rape." By that summer, the Project had agreed to represent him. That alone was a huge victory.

Branches of the Innocence Project exist nationwide to free people who have been wrongfully incarcerated. I understood how lucky we were, given that the Project only takes a few cases every year and that they have extraordinary results. They often prove a client's innocence by getting courts to order re-testing of DNA evidence. In the past two decades, Innocence Project attorneys have helped prove the innocence of well over 350 wrongly-convicted people across the country. Tuggle, I hoped, would be next.

Still, when the Ninth Circuit reached their disappointing decision, that his three-strikes sentence was not, in fact, grossly disproportionate to the crime of possessing one dose of a controlled substance, the Project had been working on the Tuggle case for almost a year. Finally, in April 2008, they filed a motion in the San Joaquin County Superior Court to have the biological samples tested for DNA. It was granted; the court ordered retesting.

I was elated. I could see myself in my typical attorney fantasy life: a black suit, my dark hair pulled back, walking slightly behind a gray-haired, white-mustached Mr. Tuggle. Together, we would stride through the gates of Folsom, moving into the blinding sun and the flashes of cameras. He and I would hug, then answer a few questions from the media. We would write a heart-wrenching but ultimately triumphant book detailing the intricacies of his case.

But the Office of the Sheriff-Coroner, the District Attorney, and the Central Valley Regional Laboratory all swore that they could not locate any biological samples. There was no DNA evidence left to test. According to the Records Division Supervisor, the records were destroyed pursuant to the "Sheriff-Coroner's Records Retention Schedule in June, 1992." The Investigations Divisions claimed that standard policy was to retain reports and records for ten years, which would have meant the DNA was discarded in 1996. Strangely, the district attorney submitted documents showing there was an order to destroy the evidence as early as 1989, only three years after Mr. Tuggle's convictions. Everyone gave a slightly different story, yet all said the same thing: the DNA evidence was gone. Lost, missing, misplaced, there was nothing to re-test and nothing to show Mr. Tuggle's innocence.

I felt, then, that innocence truly meant nothing. And I had ample evidence to back this idea. In 2014, *Proceedings of the National Academy of Sciences* published a study, "Rate of False Conviction of Criminal Defendants Who Are Sentenced to Death." It established that 4.1 percent of people sentenced to death are probably innocent. Given that there are 2,673[19] people on death row in the US as of 2019, that means approximately 109 people are scheduled to be put to death for crimes they did not commit. Applying that estimate to the 2.2 million people in prison, over 90,000 innocent people sit in cold, concrete cells right now, defeated, scared, and baffled. I imagined David Tuggle waking up every morning wondering how the hell he got there.

David Tuggle, though, responded with true twelve-step gratitude, true prisoner fatalism, and true cowboy grit: "I feel it un-American to give up trying to find some justice."

He has inspired me to find justice, too, by sharing the injustice of his convictions and the complicated fates of my other clients with more than three old guys in black robes. As the statute of limitations in Doug's case crawled toward expiration, I sat in cafés writing the last chapters of this book. I took on fewer new cases and watched old ones finally come to resolution.

I felt I was coming to the end of a long journey. When I finally started to let myself believe that Doug might not be locked away from us, it felt like I had returned home from a long trip, both a beautiful vacation on the beach where you feel tired from wind and swimming, and a visit back home where you remember the annoyances and expectations and turkey loafs of your childhood. It's exhausting. But to have survived the journey, lived it or lived

---

19 According to the Death Penalty Information Center, www.deathpenaltyinfo.org

through it, and then return home, that was the sensation I had: growth and completion and peace.

I wrote to David Tuggle to ask permission to tell his story. He and I together wouldn't write the heart-wrenching but triumphant book of his release from prison after DNA evidence proved his innocence, but I thought his story and his insights had value and could impact readers.

He was a man who had convinced me—if not the court—that he was innocent. No one could be sure, of course, because the DNA had been lost. Still, he was a victim of the three-strikes law, one that is widely held as flawed, as well as being prey to a woman who was coerced into thinking she was seeing her rapist in an innocent man. He was sitting in prison, and I figured he would have some insights into our criminal justice system, an understanding that could help me calibrate my role in the system—as an attorney, and now, as a wife and so-far survivor of the threat of prosecution.

The David Tuggle whom I remembered as tall and worn, with that graying handlebar mustache, took the time to write a letter that is among my most meaningful possessions:

I learned it's my fault. If I'd have been doing the right thing, I wouldn't have been doing the wrong thing.

I now know I had a serious drug and alcohol problem. And when [the judge] at my three strikes sentencing hearing asked me if I had ever blacked out from alcohol and/or drugs and I confessed that I had, he asked how did I know I didn't commit those rapes?

I had no answer.

Could I have committed these crimes? I couldn't answer that question for a long time. It wasn't until you got the Innocence Project involved, and we found out the evidence to prove my innocence was destroyed, that I lost all hope of redemption. I had to make a cold hard ugly decision.

For my own mind and rehabilitation, it is better to accept that I could have, during a black-out, committed the crime against Nicole D. I was under the influence enough to have acted inappropriately with Debra R, and not have a correct recollection. My admitting this will be my assurance I will never use alcohol or drugs for the rest of my life. (I have been sober and clean now for 19 years.)

If I was guilty of these crimes, I do owe many an apology. I have written a letter of apology and sent it to the Board of Parole Hearings and the California Department of Corrections. They said they posted it on their website.

I think acceptance and apology are the most important things I have done since I've been locked up, for me and for everyone.

Sincerely,

David Tuggle

I couldn't believe what he said. Maybe he wasn't innocent. He could have committed the crimes. Memory is fallible, even without drugs or alcohol. We can readily convince ourselves into believing what we want. Facing DNA testing of the evidence forced David Tuggle to acknowledge that fact.

I had believed in his innocence. I always told people that innocence didn't matter—that our legal system required zealous representation for even the guilty—and yet, I realized I had given special attention to those I thought were innocent. I had used my defense of them as a pedestal, a way to secure myself, at least in my own mind, as standing over all the spoiled, entitled government attorneys. I was a righteous hero who would save the innocent victims who happened to be convicted criminals. Suddenly, instead of Tuggle playing the victim with me as his hero, our story had become blurred, so complicated that I could not see straight.

I began to question my own innocence. I had let naiveté and privilege mask my crimes and mistakes as unoffending. I questioned the innocence of defendants who juries acquitted and who walked free. I questioned the innocence of those who were never charged because of connections or status or money. I had seen for years that guilt was messy, but now I saw that innocence was not simple either.

| | | | |

"Did you read the article in yesterday's *Chronicle*?" Cris asked me on the phone, almost three years after Doug had received the subpoena.

I hadn't had two minutes on my soccer-packed Sunday to read so much as a headline.

"I'm not an optimistic person," she said, and I smiled to myself. No attorney could be. "But I think it's good news."

The article was about bid rigging cases across the country. The Justice Department had created a special task force to prosecute bidders and buyers who had been involved with artificially lowering the prices of foreclosed homes sold on the courthouse steps. They had gotten fifty-some-odd convictions in Northern California alone. But Cris's optimism came from the line she read into the telephone:

"Federal officials say they expect to charge a few more people in the coming months, but that cases are expected to soon drop off now that the heated foreclosure market of late 2008 and 2009 has cooled."

"If the government is going to charge a few more people in the coming months,'" she said, "that means prosecutors are pretty far along in those cases. A lot more work would have to be done in Doug's case."

My voice got shaky, but I forced a whispered thank you.

She said I should come by for lunch anytime.

I had been renting an office in Cris's building for the last year, but I was moving out. I wasn't taking new clients. I had been hit too hard by losing the cases for two young men from Central California: Felipe, who at sixteen-years-old, got a life sentence for being a passenger in the car during a drive-by shooting, and Nick Yang. I found myself deeply affected by the two years I had spent defending Nick; the one-time responsible Hmong boy who loved math, who grew up in the Central Valley where I, too, had been a child, but who would be spending seventy years in a cement box in Folsom while the real shooter enjoyed his plea bargain.

I had lost those cases within months of Doug's company receiving their subpoena. In the past, I had gotten energy from small, partial victories, from my part ending shackling for juveniles, or for getting a client the custody credits he deserved for the time he spent in jail waiting for trial. I used to feel passionate about the larger idea that my work protected the Constitution. I loved arguing against warrantless police searches of personal items, and I loved fighting for juveniles thrown away into the California Youth Authority.

But with our subpoena—because, at some point I had started to think of it as *ours*—I was faced with the brutal reality that victory for Doug could mean a felony conviction and probation instead of prison. Any small win suddenly felt like defeat. The fact that I could do so little for my husband and my family—even when I was fully professionally equipped to help—made me feel shriveled, useless. In the years after Doug was served, while searching for an attorney who could possibly save us, while saying nothing to friends and neighbors, while pretending—to our kids and to everyone—that all was well, I saw that the justice system was controlled by fear, dominance, indifference, and imprisonment. I could not change any of that. I had lost my passion.

Only months after Doug had called me to say he needed a lawyer, a friend recommended me for a teaching position at Berkeley Law. This new professional avenue seemed wide and welcome, and I followed it with relief. I focused on pedagogy. I developed curriculum. There was real solace even in managing the nuts and bolts of attendance, grading, and conferences. Spiritually, the act of sharing meaningful knowledge with other people refreshed me. I began to think of appeals as reactionary. They seemed dark, negative. My clients had been pushed deep into a broken and retributive hole, and I was being dragged in after them. I did not want to abandon them, but I felt that the help I could offer wasn't as meaningful as I wanted it to be.

Standing in a classroom before fifteen dedicated, ambitious students who might change the world? That felt creative. It was positive and light. I was still helping people. My students learned about the US legal system, employment discrimination, patent protections, and crafting persuasive arguments. I helped them improve their writing, sometimes significantly, over the course of a year. Instead of menacing phone messages, my students brought me mooncakes for Chinese New Year and took pictures with me at the end of the semester. Their energy buoyed me. Teaching didn't pay well, especially for an attorney, but Doug's company had grown, and we didn't need my income as much as we had. University salary, though, definitely didn't rent an office in Cris's hip Berkeley neighborhood.

I told Doug about the article as soon as I heard him come through the creaky kitchen door. It was almost 6:30. As his father had before him, my husband always came home for dinner.

I moved from where I was stirring the polenta to the other side of the kitchen island.

"Yeah, I saw the article."

He wasn't grinning. He wasn't beaming. He didn't look nearly as relieved as I thought he would. He took off the jacket with the blue and gold company logo on the front. He looked beat.

"Listen," I said, "I talked to Cris. She said it was good news. After saying she's not one to give good news."

He looked up. Genuinely surprised, he said, "Why?"

"It said the investigation is winding down. They must have gotten everything they needed from the subpoena. They would have to be much further along in your case if they were hoping to prosecute. There was nothing in your situation to warrant any additional . . . anything!"

"But. It says it's still going on. The investigation."

"Only for a few more months. They haven't so much as talked to you guys. No follow-up. None. Which means they're focused on the people who really are involved in that mess."

Doug stared at me for a long second. His arms came up toward me, as his head started to sag. When he pulled me to him, I could feel the warmth of his blue button-down. He smelled like wood and vanilla; he smelled the same, after all these years.

"Honestly?" he said. "I hadn't thought about it for a while, then yesterday I read the paper. I didn't sleep at all last night."

"It's going to be okay."

Again, he pulled me to him and I felt his weight, the density of his body, the years of worry.

Stepping back, looking at me with his bright green eyes, he said, "Not that it's officially over. I don't know when it will be. Doesn't matter, maybe. Because something you told me a while back has stuck with me."

I had no idea what he would say. I didn't realize he listened to me so closely.

"Remember when I was so mad? At first? I was so worried it would ruin the company if investors and analysts and lawyers blew it out of proportion."

How could I forget the evening in bed with the curtains drawn, the other nights of sleeplessness, his fury at the lawyers, at the feeling that his company would fail, that he would be made out to be a criminal, that he would be taken away from us?

"You told me that wasn't the right way to look at it. There was a better way. It was highly possible that the company would never be where it is now—about to be publicly traded—if it weren't for the investigation. It put a fire under us. We needed to show everyone that we had a real business, a solid outfit that contributed to the community."

I *had* told him that. I had said those words when it looked like he and Colin would have to stop leading their company because of the subpoena. Just as their livelihood, their baby, was growing up and beginning to flourish, they would have to give it away. But there might not have been anything to give away without that subpoena. Doug had succeeded—not *despite* the threat of criminal charges, but *because* of it.

"I can't believe it," he said. "It's impossible. To believe this truly happened to us and that it turned out the way it did."

"It's the truth. The whole crazy truth." And with a tighter embrace, I told my husband with certainty, "We're going to make it."

Lance Jones didn't make it. He might have committed suicide in his jail cell or been stabbed in an episode with another desperate inmate. It could have been a heart attack or a drug overdose. We don't know how, but Lance Jones died in jail waiting for attempted murder charges to play out against him.

Late in 2017, while he was out on bail awaiting sentencing on his federal convictions for bid rigging, Lance and his girlfriend spent the evening at a local casino. I resist the temptation to decide, definitively, that a divorced, bankrupt, and unemployed Lance had turned to gambling in desperation to earn the money to pay the fines associated with his conviction, to pay for rent and food. Doug had denied him work and had rejected his thinly-veiled extortion attempt. But we could not have imagined how acute Lance's problems had become.

According to local newspapers, the couple allegedly stalked a fifty-five-year-old Fremont woman around the casino, then followed her home. As the woman fumbled with her keys at her front door, Lance approached from behind and struck her head with a flashlight before taking her purse and departing in a tan car. Shortly after the attack, investigators went to the casino, where surveillance video showed a man, identified by security guards as forty-four-year-old Lance Jones, shadowing the victim around the casino floor. Officers later searched Lance's girlfriend's home in the East Bay, where they found a Maglite flashlight and the victim's wallet, identification, credit cards, and purse.

The picture of Lance in the newspaper—probably a mug shot—looked like an emaciated shell of a street thug. Sunken cheeks, gray skin, greased hair. Once again, I remembered Doug's company barbeque in our backyard, the first and only time I met Lance. Smiling and tanned, he shook my hand and thanked us for inviting his whole family. His mother-in-law was visiting from out-of-town, and he'd hoped it was all right that they'd brought her.

Doug and I had been *this close* to a fate like Lance's, with his long, surfer shorts and slicked-back hair, his blonde wife and his two innocent kids. T*his close* to a spiraling disaster of mistakes, then lies, then convictions, followed by desperation, then maybe drugs and finally death. We were *this close*—and yet, for us, everything, *everything* is different.

He may be in prison still, but David Tuggle is a different person, too. Prison gave him the gift of time. Prison gives inmates endless hours for thinking about mistakes, for considering how our families and environments and choices shape us, for reflecting on this convoluted legal system. It also gives people time to read, to study, to educate themselves. Tuggle now helps other inmates navigate the system with his near-professional legal skills. I have to imagine he also helps others maintain the sobriety that is the source of such pride. Though all my clients helped me, it feels like David Tuggle most clearly taught me about the contradictions and the complications at the core of our system.

The legal system in the United States ultimately does not rest on justice versus injustice. Nor do verdicts depend on guilt versus innocence. The criminal justice system is as strange and imperfect as the people who comprise it. I am not exempt; I have made careless mistakes and stupid choices. The stories in this book—those of my clients, their families, the attorneys and judges, the victims—have built this system. But our story is not the triumph of the good or the punishment of the evil. Our story is about poverty and greed, miscommunications and uninformed choices, privilege and powerlessness, failures and fears. Our stories are about courage, remorse, and perseverance. As David Tuggle said, our stories must be about apologies and acceptance.

No apology can free Nick Yang, even after Pao Ma admitted to having done the shooting. Pao served one-seventh of the time that Nick will. This is the kind of thing I think about when pushing through a door into bright California sunshine. It's what I think about when I tell my kids to have a good day and watch them race out the back gate.

I can only hope that Nick will find acceptance.

I have told Nick's story, the one the jury never heard. I have spoken of Jake Mendoza, who didn't understand his plea agreement and had an attorney who wouldn't explain it. Deshaun, who was pinned to cold concrete and shackled in court for stealing a bottle of NyQuil. Deandra, who may have been involved in some way with a horrible shooting but who may have been innocent and who spent seven years away from her kids anyway. Fetu Faraimo, my proudest victory, but a man who still spent twenty years in prison. Each of his five kids is an adult now.

Perhaps someone someday will hear Nick's story, remember him, and want to fix this system of plea bargains, power plays, and aggressive prosecutions, all of which shape the criminal justice system. And just as Barbara Babcock taught me at Stanford, I remain convinced that telling people the human story behind the label "criminal" has the power to change the world.

Perhaps justice for David Tuggle *was* his three-strikes conviction for possessing one dose of meth. His conviction and its staggering sentence gave him the time in prison to face what he had done or might have done. He faced his life, his addiction, his choices. And perhaps I helped him find some measure of honesty and absolution by telling his story to the Ninth Circuit, by getting the Innocence Project to take his case, and by helping him take the first few steps that led to the apology to the victims.

Perhaps there was a certain kind of "justice" for Doug in this subpoena. His time under investigation helped clarify what really mattered to him. Instead of pursuing the next super-human career accomplishment or driving us all up yet another dusty mountain trail only to find another rocky cliff, now Doug appreciates each day with our three children. He is thankful for his mostly-sane wife, her darn good dinners, and for relaxing in the hot tub together on a Sunday afternoon. Maybe I helped him get there, by vividly drawing the worst-case scenarios, by staying with him on bumpy roads, by easing him out of the NFL so he could find even bigger successes, by loving our kids, as beautiful and imperfect as they might be.

Perhaps I have come to the right ending for my story. I gave every client my most passionate, well-researched, well-written self. But those clients gave me even more. I had been a little girl wracked with abandonment and self-doubt, a girl who didn't fit in anywhere. I failed to use my voice to protect my body, and I defended immoral corporations. As a wife and mother, I almost drowned in tedium and stress. I almost lost my sense of self completely. Before defending criminals, I was naïve and scared, but also entitled and unappreciative. Through their drug trafficking and their aggravated assaults, their robberies and sometimes violent murders, my clients showed me that I was an independent, powerful person. I was also broken and flawed. Ultimately, I was human, just like them.

Justice is finding your better self in the face of mistakes. Justice is admitting the truths about yourself—both your innocent mistakes and more malicious ones—then accepting them. Justice is embracing your own concrete box, whatever shape it might take.

ABOUT THE AUTHOR

Shanti Brien has a bachelor's degree in ethnic studies from UC Berkeley and a JD from Stanford Law School. She is an accomplished criminal defense attorney with a specialty in appeals and post-conviction proceedings. She is co-founder of Fogbreak Justice, an education and consulting company with the mission to transform the criminal justice system through experiences that reduce bias, promote fairness, build community trust, and create equity. Shanti writes about criminal justice and other social justice issues on Medium @shantibrightbrien. She co-authored *June Jordan's Poetry for the People: A Revolutionary Blueprint* (Routledge, 1995), and contributed to *The Road to Independence: 101 Women's Journeys to Starting Their Own Law Firms* (American Bar Association, 2011) and *Lose the Cape: The Mom's Guide to Becoming Socially and Politically Engaged* (Kat Biggie Press, 2018). She lives in the East Bay with her husband and three kids.